LIFE'S TOO F***ING SHORT...

C O N T E N T S

LIFE'S TOO F**ING SHORT to get depressed about being

* FORTY-SOMETHING * FRIENDLESS * BROKE

I am a great believer in the power of positive thinking, and not expecting that life will be 'lucky'. How I hate that word, especially when people come up to me and say 'you've had some lucky breaks in your career'. No, I didn't. WOMEN DON'T GET LUCKY BREAKS. We are rewarded for working twice as hard as men to get noticed, for juggling all the competing bits of our lives. LUCK DOESN'T COME INTO IT. If we get a better job or a pay rise, it's because WE'VE WORKED OUR SOCKS OFF for it.

There's no point in getting bitter and twisted about this — that's the way it is. And don't bother picking up a magazine and feeling that everything in your life doesn't seem as interesting as what's going on in celebrity world. Be honest, do you want to be photographed every time you put out the rubbish or go to get a newspaper? Do you want to be telling journalists about how you've spent a load of money having your nose rebuilt? How your best friends are a bunch of gay men, your cleaner is Ukrainian, and how you're never going to have kids? Too much information! Some celebrities are truly addicted to fame and feel that they have to include us – the public – in everything they think and do. Or they moan about a 'lack of privacy' while beaming down at us from every billboard flogging everything from eyeliner to handbags, getting paid a million pounds a deal.

Since I appeared on *I'm A Celebrity…*, people recognise me everywhere I go. It's fine – I couldn't care less. I was well paid and raised a lot of money for charity. I'm not going to whinge on about people checking out my basket in supermarkets (I buy toilet rolls because I crap like normal people), or complain because someone calls out my name at an airport. I don't even get pissed off with men in white vans imitating my accent – because, at the end of the day they are sad, paunchy chaps sitting in cheap white vans, and I am swanning about in a taxi paid for by a film company and I live in a nice house. If they were any good at impersonations I presume they would be on telly or the radio, and not mending pipes or carrying boxes all day.

I can write this book because I grew up weird looking, with big frilly teeth, thick glasses and boring hair. I was the girl who never had a boyfriend at school, the last one in the class to wear a bra, the girl others used to call 'lezzie' in the changing rooms for netball. Externally I might have seemed gauche and insecure, but inside I knew I was special and different. I've always had a huge amount of self-belief. Sure, it was tempered with a healthy dollop of insecurity brought about by my looks and my accent, and the fact that from the moment I was on the radio and then on television the critics loved to try and slag me off as much as possible. But instead of letting it get me down, I just got stronger.

DECODE THE TWADDLE
BEAMED AT YOU EVERY DAY

We are assaulted with advice on every side, from fashion and beauty writers to 'tips' from celebrities. Newspapers and magazines now give a large amount of space, not just to advice columnists, but also to 'life' gurus, and advisers who lecture us on everything from diet to ethical living. The end result, after reading the Saturday or Sunday papers, with all their supplements, is utter exhaustion and a sense of confusion and inadequacy.

A huge industry has grown up that purports to 'help' women, but in my opinion just does the complete opposite.

How many times have you found a little stack of scraps of newsprint, perhaps 'useful' addresses culled from magazines, pushed under the phone book or a vase? Honestly, you could spend hours every week online – making friends, ordering organically, checking out designer fashion. You could spend half a day a week (and a considerable sum of money) on the latest beauty treatments, trying to stave off the inevitable ageing process. You could cross the country sourcing organic, hand-reared ingredients to make perfect suppers. OR YOU COULD HAVE A LIFE. I am trying to wean myself off this addiction – hoarding cuttings listing who does the 'ultimate facial', where to buy the 'best hand-made pasta', or where to source 'jeans that flatter every figure'.

ADOPT A HEALTHY CYNICISM ABOUT SO-CALLED EXPERTS

Once experts had qualifications and certificates, but now they are self-appointed gurus who specialise in everything from reading the irises of our eyes to the state of our large intestines. You can call up parenting experts, eco-auditors, feng shui experts, wardrobe advisers, and people who come around and de-clutter your home, chucking stuff in bin bags. I feel weak just reading about this army of experts who can (for a hefty fee) sort out my life and hopefully make me feel calmer and less stressed. But it's all bollocks of course . . .

I was reading an article the other day, entitled 'How To Be Happy'. Apparently there is an equation that defines this: $H=S+C+V$, where $H=$Happiness, S is the biological point at which you feel happy, C is the conditions of your life, and V the voluntary choices we make. Confused? I certainly was. Especially when the writer went on to talk about the perfect conditions to produce happiness, defining them as Peace and Quiet, Relationships, and Sharing. TALK ABOUT STATING THE BLOODY OBVIOUS. Of course it is important to have some reflective time in your life, but the right sounds (like music) can make you happy, ecstatic and uplifted. Relationships – obviously a good relationship is ideal, but do you know anyone who would ever define their most important relationship as anything other than difficult? Let's be realistic, the best thing about relationships is not to let them dominate your life or penetrate your inner psyche. Sharing – well, that goes without saying, but there's a fine line between sharing and being drained. At the end of reading this 'expert' view I was more than a bit cross that I'd wasted ten minutes trying to understand a theory that seemed full of holes. In the end, we can all be as happy or as miserable as we want – **if we feel miserable, only we can resolve that,** not an expert, not a bloke, not a pill, not an alternative treatment and definitely not a face cream.

Talking of treatments, I read about one the other day in which you put yourself in a compartment chilled to minus 135 degrees – that's six times colder than a domestic freezer! This is cryotherapy, and its advocates claim that it stimulates all our bodily functions, improving circulation and our immune response. The writer said it improves skin quality, 'clearing away lactic acid and toxins'. STOP RIGHT THERE! A 'holistic' doctor claimed 'it is as though our healing response has become dormant only to be reawakened instantly'. A BMA spokesman told the writer 'it is not inconceivable that reduced temperatures might have quite substantial side effects'.

WHEN YOU ANALYSE THE TWADDLE THAT PASSES FOR INFORMED COPY IN WOMEN'S MAGAZINES THESE DAYS, YOU FIND GLARING HOLES.

The BMA bloke used the word 'might'. And he didn't use the word 'benefits' as a by-product of the treatment, but used the far more cautious term 'side effects'. The journalist claimed that she felt 'elated' after her three-minute session, which cost a whopping £30. I am sure that a lot of alternative therapies, like massage and acupuncture, do give huge benefits – but they don't work for everyone. What I thoroughly object to is the presentation of this stuff as if it were unassailable truth, when in fact it often just fills up space under the guise of telling us about the latest must-have treatment.

We are being offered more kinds of beauty products, more kinds of therapies like this than ever. The net result of all this choice? Three-quarters of all women in their thirties and forties say they are lucky to get six hours of sleep a night and many say they feel tired all the time. A survey found that a whopping fifty-nine per cent of women over thirty said they felt tired 'all the time', and only one in twelve ate a proper breakfast, getting through the day eating snacks rather than meals. Now an increasing number of women get headaches, eczema, chest infections and heart palpitations – all manifestations of the stressed lives they lead.

Life's too short for all of this.

SOMEHOW WE MUST IMPROVE OUR QUALITY OF LIFE, BUT **IT IS UP TO US** TO PRIORITISE, STOP DOING SOME THINGS AND FIND TIME FOR OURSELVES.

The current situation is a sad reflection of our attempts to have it all and in the end our health suffers. You can chuck money at quick-fix solutions like beauty treatments, but in truth, you need to have a radical rethink.

THE MOST IMPORTANT PERSON IN YOUR LIFE – THE PERSON WHO SETS THE RULES, DECIDES THE AGENDA, CHUCKS OUT THE MENTAL AND PHYSICAL DETRITUS – **IS YOU.**

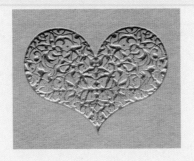

WHEN YOU WAKE UP,
LIE STILL FOR TWO MINUTES

Recite over and over again:

I AM BLOODY BRILLIANT.

I AM GREAT.

I AM NUMBER ONE.

UNIQUE.

I LIKE ME.

I AM WORTH IT.

I AM HIGHLY INTELLIGENT,
NO MATTER WHAT OTHERS MAY SAY.

You have to do this, because, take it from me, no one else is ever going to tell you that in the coming twenty-four hours. To value myself is the single most important thing I have learned over the years. No one ever did me a favour. No one ever gave me a career break out of pity. I did it all for myself. By believing in myself.

SET AN AGENDA,
AND WRITE A SHORT LIST
BEFORE YOU GO TO BED
EVERY NIGHT

Do not put more than five or six things on it – any more would be unrealistic. On a day-to-day basis, don't make lists you can't achieve. You should not carry over more than a couple of things to the next day's list. At the same time, stop and spend a few hours alone, making a plan for yourself.

DECIDE WHAT YOU ARE NOT GOING TO DO ANY MORE

* the people you are not going to call back ✔
* the books you will never read ✔
* the relatives you can send to social Siberia ✔
* the food you are not going to cook ✔
* the man/men you're not going to wait on hand
  and foot any more ✔
* the clothes you will not buy ✔
* the stuff you don't need ✔
* the boring job you're not going to suffer any longer ✔

Plan your time to make sure that every week you set aside a slot for stuff that you want to do – grow lettuces on the windowsill, go to evening classes, join a walking club, learn another language, plan an activity holiday with people you don't know. Hopefully this book will give you a starting point. Establish you own rules and stick to them. Good luck!

unpromising raw material!

LIFE'S TOO F***ING SHORT TO SPEND £100 ON FACE CREAM

thin me 1997 never achieved since

- Ignore beauty journalists
- Make the most of what you've got
- How to find a great hairdresser

Why do intelligent women have shelves of rotting makeup?

Why are so-called beauty writers lying cows?

Why is most expensive face cream a waste of money?

Why is there so much pressure to have cosmetic surgery?

Why bother to read 'top tips' coming from the famous?

IT'S WHY-OH-WHY TIME

IF THE BEAUTY INDUSTRY HAD TO GO THROUGH THE KIND OF CHECKS IMPOSED ON THE CARS WE DRIVE OR THE FOOD WE EAT, IT WOULD GO OUT OF BUSINESS.

Has there ever been such a massive industry built entirely on wishful thinking? Just as nine women out of ten aren't happy with the shape of their bodies, four out of five of us think that in a laboratory somewhere a miracle worker of a scientist is going to come up with a cream that will stop the ageing process, iron out wrinkles, tighten up flabby chins and take a decade off our appearances if we slavishly slather it on day in and day out. **THERE IS NO SUCH CREAM AND PROBABLY NEVER WILL BE.** While there may be a raft of rules and regulations ensuring that the products we put on our skin do not actually harm us, there is nothing to ensure that they will actually deliver what they promise. The food industry is strictly regulated, and recently Flora was ordered to alter their advertising so that they could only claim that their spreads lowered your cholesterol as *part* of a healthy regime involving diet and exercise. No such tight controls seem to operate when it comes to the ludicrous claims we read in ads for face cream, anti-cellulite gel, and skin-brightening products.

From the age of eleven I worshipped at the altar of self-improvement.

Didn't we all? Given the raw material of my genetic inheritance it wasn't surprising that I looked in the mirror and felt miserable. I had big, sticky-out teeth, National Health glasses like milk-bottle bottoms, long legs like sticks, a completely flat chest and beige hair. Hair that lay flat on my head, and wasn't the slightest bit interested in being wavy, curly or interesting.

When I was smaller my mother would tear up strips of old sheets and tie my hair in rags, night after night. Soon I suffered from acute sleep deprivation – it was like sleeping on a bag of marbles. Every morning Mum would unwrap these tight twirls of cotton, and hey presto – my hair sank limply onto my head, straight but with a weird kink halfway down.

By the time I was fourteen I was determined to go blonde in the name of glamour, but dyed hair was forbidden at school. In desperation I noticed that new brands of toothpaste were emblazoned 'with added peroxide', and so I would sit in class, TOOTHPASTE TUBE IN HAND hidden under the desk, METHODICALLY RUBBING COLGATE INTO MY HAIR for hours at a time. After a few weeks it resembled a set of matted dreadlocks, but when I washed off the accumulated gunk, I was left with the same flat, boring beige hair I'd had before I started. It was a sad day!

Next, I bought a spray to dye my hair silver and used that whenever I went out clubbing. It was fine, so long as no one actually touched my head, as it came straight off.

I tried false fingernails and was embarrassed when dancing with a cute boy and they dropped off, like nasty bird talons, in his hand. I got fabulous false eyelashes, but I didn't glue them on very carefully and they would eventually start to come off and droop over my eyes like sagging venetian blinds. Once I shagged a well-known artist after he'd given a lecture at Cambridge University – in the morning I found my false eyelashes lying on the sheets, like a couple of dead furry caterpillars. I prayed that he hadn't seen them.

Over the years I changed my glasses and my hair more than most people change their underwear. The results were generally horrible – and when I am on my deathbed I intend to summon all the shit hairdressers I have paid over the years and read them the riot act. I have had pink hair, orange hair, black and white extensions, a yellow star dyed in my hair and dreary blonde streaks. It's been bobbed, cropped, and left to fester for two years, long and lank.

Why oh why does it take twenty years of failures to find a haircut that works?

Here's my advice: forget everything you read about fashionable hairstyles, there's only ever going to be one that works on your head anyway. Why I grew my hair long I do not know, because I have no idea how to put it up or style it in any way. It was probably because I couldn't face telling my hairdresser that I didn't like the way he cut my hair, but because he was so nice I couldn't face sacking him! I spent two years walking around with my hair in a bulldog clip because it was hot and heavy. Loads and loads of women have exactly the same relationship with their hairdressers – sick isn't it? Hair is such a barometer of your inner turmoil, and when you go to the hairdressers, and they start to snip at your fringe, don't you just start to panic? It's as if you've been caught out shopping without any underwear on… most of us use our hair as a versatile way of hiding at least a third of our faces. A short fringe makes you feel naked. Hairdressing salons are places of utter misery.

LIFE'S TOO SHORT TO HAVE YOUR HAIR DONE BY SOMEONE WHO HASN'T A CLUE.

Don't you just know as they start to blow dry, that it's all going to come out wrong? My palms start sweating, and before long I start to feel queasy. I have walked out of more hairdressers with wet hair than I want to remember. The thing is, they are practising on you – they are not the people who have to go home and live with the result. Mostly, they couldn't give a flying f***, and the best you can hope for is ten per cent of their concentration. They are generally bored and you aren't interesting or famous enough to engage them. If I go to a salon where I have never been before, I always ask the youngest junior to blow dry my hair – at least they'll have their finger on the pulse of what's happening, as opposed to some bitter old senior stylist.

THE PHOTOS OF ME OVER THE YEARS ARE LIVING PROOF THAT A HAIRDRESSER CAN BE A WOMAN'S WORST ENEMY.

I'm tall, so why would I want really short hair unless I am as skinny as top model Agyness Deynn? Unless you are a size ten, once you pass thirty, and are taller than average, just forget getting your hair cropped, no matter what your hairdresser claims. You will just look like a scout mistress or a clothes peg.

Let's talk about that stuff hairdressers call 'products'. What is this gunk they slather on? It's called things like MUD, LIFT, ANTI-FRIZZ, RELAXANT, VOLUME CONTROL – all totally mystifying. I culled the following product names from a recent magazine feature about stuff that claims to make your hair shine more: LAMINATE WEIGHTLESS SHINE..... VOLUMIZING POLISH..... POLISHING MILK.....

IT'S GOBBLEDEGOOK

COLOUR SHINE BRIGHTENER LOTION... PROFESSIONAL LUMINOUS MASK.... ANTI-AGEING POLISHING SERUM..... ILLUMINATING SHAMPOO.

Confused? We've got serums, gels, masks, milk, shampoo and polish – which all proves that very few hairdressers achieved A-level English. I guarantee that if your hairdresser puts loads of different 'products' on your hair, you will never achieve the same look at home. And if the end result in the salon involves complicated blow drying or – my idea of complete hell – the use of rollers, forget it.

Hairdressers talk a whole load of bollocks about what they are slapping on your hair – it's all designed to get you back through their door on a weekly basis.

By the way, the reason why my hair always looks really shiny – it's dyed! God knows what horrible grey colour exists under the bucket of red vegetable colouring that gets dumped on it every three weeks. I certainly am not interested in the natural look, nor should any woman be over the age of forty! So how do you get great hair?

PURE AND SIMPLE.

Life's too short to visit the hairdresser every seven days – are you made of money?

I have to have hair that looks good for filming and television work. It has taken me **THIRTY YEARS** to find a nice, non-egotistical hairdresser who comes around to my house on his scooter, cuts, dyes and blow dries my hair in record time. Whatever he costs is cheaper and less stressful than schlepping to a salon on the other side of London, buying cups of coffee, being charged for a glass of water, and listening to some skinny bitch in the chair next to you whingeing about her au pair, her cleaner, her nanny. Now I have hair that looks the same week in and week out – perfect! It's cut so that I can wash it, rub my head with a towel, and it comes out approximately the same. Try to get a hairdresser you know and trust to come around to your home or office after work, and get a couple of friends to combine their appointments with yours. That way the stylist can make a decent amount of money, and you can all sit around having something to eat and a drink. That way, getting your hair done is fun. And here's my ultimate tip: **LIFE'S TOO SHORT TO WASH YOUR HAIR MORE THAN ONCE A WEEK.**

When I appeared on *I'm a Celebrity...* in the Australian jungle, my hairdresser gave me an excellent piece of advice: don't wash your hair. For three weeks all I ever did was splash it with cold water in order to damp down the smell of the fire I did the cooking on. Hair cleans itself – and after a limp couple of days it sorts itself out and actually feels thicker and has more body. It didn't go frizzy, the colour didn't fade in the sun – in short it looked far better than I did wearing horrible baggy shorts and a red fleece with 'JSP' and a phone number emblazoned across my back. When I go on holiday, or when I'm travelling and not filming or doing television, I only wash my hair once a week at the most. And I never, ever wash it more than once, I use the minimum amount of shampoo and never use conditioner. You need to cut right back on the crap you use – it all piles up and makes hair lank, and doesn't allow it to sort itself out naturally. The only reason I wash my hair more often is if I've been in a room or club with smokers – but as they are banned from more or less everywhere now, that is relatively rare. And, after filming in an abattoir for *The F-Word* on a couple of occasions – the smell of freshly slaughtered carcasses sticks to absolutely everything and I had to wash everything I was wearing, too.

LIFE'S TOO SHORT TO SPEND A FORTUNE ON FACE CREAM. I

am sixty, and I might be a bit lumpy around the midriff, but I have great skin – it's one of the few things I can sincerely thank my late mother for. I have small wrinkles around my eyes, bags under them after a late night and a saggy chin, but as I talk a huge amount on the telly you probably don't have time to notice these minor deficiencies! Every day of my life someone compliments me on my skin and says I don't look my age. Well, I do look my age if I feel miserable, am sulking or falling asleep, believe me!

Women often ask what is the secret of good skin – apart from genetics – and it is simple, but so hard to achieve:

* not smoking
* refusing class-A drugs
* drinking loads of water
* sleeping at least six hours a night
* wearing sunblock
* enjoying life (miseries do look wrinkly, don't they?)

I look at the Duchess of Cornwall, younger than me, with horrible pleats all around her mouth from puffing on dozens of cigarettes a day for decades. Even if she's given up now to please Charles, it's too late, the damage has been done. Ditto sunbathing. Luckily I wore specs all the time until I was in my fifties, which protected the skin around my eyes from wind. I also wore sunglasses in bright light to avoid screwing my eyes up too much, still do. Now I have had my eyes lasered they are more exposed – I haven't got glasses to hide behind, but my wrinkles are relatively fine.

It doesn't matter what crap is written on the tube of eye cream, once you've got wrinkles they are not going to go away.

What do you want the cream to do – turn into thread and make a giant pleat in your face? I have facials every couple of months but, quite honestly, it's more a way of lying down, being pampered and having my eyebrows and facial hair dealt with than any radical improvement on my appearance. Facials aren't going to change your skin overnight. But beauticians (who are generally ordinary working girls and not over-paid beauty writers who get loads of freebies) do give out some top tips. One told me to alternate cheap face cream with expensive gunk, as your skin gets used to any kind of cream. I use the Bharti Vyas Skin Wisdom range from Tesco, none of which costs more that £10 – and I guarantee it gets the same results as moisturisers like Crème de La Mer at £80 and more a pot.

THE TRICK WITH SKIN CARE IS TO KEEP IT VERY SIMPLE. GET UP, WASH YOUR FACE WITH CREAM OR CLEANSER, EVERY SINGLE DAY (I HAVE NEVER USED SOAP ON MY FACE SINCE I WAS FOURTEEN). PUT ON MOISTURISER. PUT SOME CRÈME OR GEL AROUND YOUR EYES. THAT'S IT.

Every night I cleanse my face even if I am so drunk I can't talk.

I slap on moisturiser and eye cream, hit the pillow. That is the sum total of my so-called beauty regime. If ever I am tempted to use some of the anti-ageing crap I'm sent, I can guarantee you that within a week the area around my eyes starts to go red, my skin begins to itch and feel over-sensitive. On the odd occasion that I have let a beauty therapist scour my skin (or exfoliate, as they call it), it will be sore the next day. Facials bring out spots you never knew you had.

I never wear foundation or thick makeup, just tinted moisturiser. **POWDER IS TOTALLY AGEING IF YOU ARE OVER FORTY.** I wear eye makeup, pencil and shadow (mascara and liner if I'm working or at a 'do') and lipstick. Takes five minutes. **TOO MUCH CACK ON YOUR SKIN WILL RUIN IT.** If a makeup artist puts base on my face because it looks washed out in the bright lights of a television studio, I remove it the minute I leave the studio.

Such a lot of drivel is written about 'hydrating' your skin. You cannot put water back into your skin no matter what you might read. All creams do is enable your skin to feel softer and more oily, not wetter. They can contain sun-block, which is good, too. But no one wants to make it sound that basic, do they? One beauty writer wrote the other day about a problem I must admit I had never thought of for one nano-second of my sixty years: 'ageing metal that lurks in your skin'. She went on to say: 'chelating agents such as lactobionic acid and gluconolactone (both new PHAs) are said to capture free iron in upper skin layers and reduce its oxidising, and therefore ageing, potential'. If you can understand that DRIVEL then you must be a top scientist. The key lies in the inclusion of the words 'are said to', which means, in a nutshell, that the manufacturers of the creams she's talking about, ie plugging (which cost £34 and £100 a pot), have made these claims, and she doesn't know whether or not there is any real scientific evidence to support a dotty theory that metal is lurking in our skin and needs to be removed with expensive cream. And does anyone outside the rarefied corridors of beauty magazines actually commonly use the word 'chelation' – which means, according to my dictionary, the treatment of heavy-metal (ie lead) poisoning?

HOW NOT TO HAVE BAGS UNDER YOUR EYES.

Feeling particularly tired one day I made an appointment with a top cosmetic surgeon who specialised in removing the bags under your eyes by making an incision that would hardly be seen.... He took one look at me and told me I needed a full face lift as well to deal with my sagging chin. It cost £750 for that consultation and the basic operation for my bags would have cost £7,000. I felt repulsive after 30 minutes of talking to this patronising man. A month later, I went on holiday, didn't take my computer, stopped drinking half a bottle of wine a day and slept properly. The bags under my eyes reduced by half immediately and I spent the £7,000 I had saved on having my garden landscaped. Hoorah! Once you go down the Botox route there's no turning back. The way I look at it, a lot of cosmetic surgery is more to do with psychological problems and general insecurities than anything else. The surgical removal of the bags under my eyes would not get me a better sex life, it would not get rid of my fat stomach and it certainly wouldn't get me better, higher-paid work. And the chances are that within a couple of years I would need to have the operation done all over again.

Face lifts have to be re-done regularly, and soon you will start to look like a startled goldfish –

like many expressionless rich American women I know, with no ear lobes and whose age can only really be determined by looking at the backs of their hands and their neck. Once you start injecting your face with Botox and fillers, then you have embarked upon a process that is highly addictive in itself. Too many women expect these procedures to give them benefits outside the purely visual. As for attending 'Botox evenings' – forget it. Why bow to peer pressure? It is a tough decision to take, at a time when the price of cosmetic surgery and minor procedures is coming down, but deep down, I do think you have to accept the ageing process and it's effect on your face. A mobile, active face will always seem more youthful, and you can certainly do facial exercises if you think they will tighten your jaw line – just don't let anyone see you.

WE ARE BOMBARDED WITH UNREALISTIC IMAGES OF OTHER WOMEN AND THEREFORE FEEL WE DON'T MAKE THE GRADE.

On my desk is a page torn from the beauty section of a best-selling women's glossy magazine. The journalist is describing something called the 'Ultimate Face Lift Treatment', which costs a whopping £450 for the first appointment. Apparently this experience involves 'a combination of bipolar radio frequency and optical energy (either laser or light)'. So far we are in mumbo jumbo land. Her face was zapped with these rays (I assume on a free treatment), a procedure which, according to her, 'heats the dermal tissue to 55 degrees and stimulates collagen production, to tighten the skin'. But how does she know? Five sessions are recommended – in other words a whopping £2,000!!! The photograph on this page is not of the journalist in question, but shows a moonlit beauty aged about eighteen, with alabaster-smooth skin, bathed in dew and tinted soft blue.

Get a grip, girls – airbrushing is commonplace in the world of beauty mythology and women's magazines. It is thoroughly evil. It just makes readers feel inferior and inadequate. This is unattainable perfection.

We all live real lives, with noisy kids, irritating partners, demanding jobs. We don't live in airbrush world, and it is always a shock to meet anyone very famous, because you see them as they really are, and not how some magazine editor would like to project them. From Elle Macpherson to Kelly Osbourne to Kate Winslet to Sienna Miller – all look normal, albeit very attractive, in the flesh – and, to be fair, all have said that they don't like being altered in this way. Look at the cover of any women's magazine – the face gazing out at you will have been doctored by an airbrush technician, removing wrinkles and sags better than any cream could ever do. And yet the result is presented to us as reality, something that we should aspire to. It makes me feel physically ill, and is causing a whole generation of young women to grow up with a warped idea of what their bodies and their faces should look like. Recently, two makeup companies have been found guilty of manipulating the truth about mascara… using fake eyelashes and airbrushing in their adverts. You'd never get the same look by just slathering on their products.

Beauty editors – how do they sleep at night? Traitors to their sex, the lot of them!

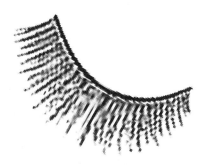

LIFE'S TOO F***ING SHORT TO TRY TO BE A SIZE ZERO

- How to eat so you are in control of your body
- How to exercise without realising it
- How to achieve a body image that is realistic

I promise you that diets never work in the long term. There is plenty of evidence demonstrating conclusively that most fatties go back to being fatties in the long run, even if they embark on a diet and initially lose a large amount of weight. Gradually our bodies learn to adapt and our metabolism will override any restricted eating plans that have been foisted on it. All those pounds you crash-dieted off in the beginning will gradually go back on – until you end up just five or six pounds lighter than when you were at your fattest. Believe me, I've been there. The trick is not to let your weight gradually accumulate in the first place, because getting rid of it is increasingly difficult as you get older. Our body shapes are determined by genetics and it is only possible to alter them within a small range.

The tough fact is that you cannot fundamentally change your body shape unless you do one of two things. The most radical solution is to spend a lot of money and opt for cosmetic surgery – and the truth is that relying on liposuction to remove fat is no long-term solution as it will just go back on in a couple of years and you'll have to have the same operation – which is major surgery – all over again. Do we really want our bodies to be scarred and dimpled where all those chips and donuts have been siphoned out?

Secondly, you can adopt the same mindset as Madonna. This woman ruthlessly exercises and works out and watches everything she eats in order to maintain a toned physique and cheat the ageing process. She looks amazing for someone in their late forties who has had a couple of kids. The only giveaway is her hands – she might have regular facials and probably has had subtle non-invasive tightening around her chin – but if you want to know how she's really ageing, look at the backs of her hands. Now her arms are starting to look stringy from years of lifting weights and those punishing routines in the gym. Do you think that Madonna looks like a woman who is having a lot of fun? No she doesn't. She's working in the entertainment business where rising young female stars like Amy Winehouse, Joss Stone and Lily Allen are in their twenties. She's a perfectionist, determined to present the best image possible at all times. Madge doesn't really do casual. I've met her a few times and we've had dinner – she's highly intelligent, but lacking in humour. She doesn't really inhabit our world, with mess, food binges and the odd bottle of wine too many. She's organised, focused, disciplined. That's why she's worth hundreds of millions of dollars and we're not. But, let's be honest – isn't it a hell of a lot more fun to sit in a bar with a girlfriend downing a bottle of sauvignon blanc, laughing and joking and eating a steak? Or would you rather be drinking a bowl of miso soup and chewing each mouthful of steamed fish fifty times in pursuit of the perfect arse?

Life's too short to start every day with three grapefruit segments, a cup of black coffee and a couple of nuts.

THE KEY TO OUR RELATIONSHIP WITH FOOD AND IT'S IMPACT ON OUR BODIES IS MODERATION, AND REALISM ABOUT WHAT IS ACHIEVABLE.

I have been to health farms – or spas as they are now known – many times. I've been away to group events where I gave up booze, did yoga and sat through lectures on how to concoct slimming salad dressings. I've detoxed. I've had colonic irrigation. I've sweated in Turkish baths and saunas. I've had sadistic beauticians wrap me in freezing gel and slather me with boiling volcanic mud in the hope of slenderising my thighs. I have religiously read every diet printed in a national newspaper over the last two decades. **I HAVE STARVED MYSELF OVER A WEEKEND**, given up tea, coffee, sugar, salt, carbs, wheat and dairy, all at different times and in different combinations.

WHAT THE HELL FOR? WHAT F***ING MYTHICAL SLENDER VERSION OF JSP WAS I DREAMING OF MORPHING INTO?

I have paid out hundreds of pounds to dieticians and nutritionists I've read about in *Vogue* who've ordered me to spend even more money on bottles of special oils and potions. They've made me put drops of various tinctures in water before every meal. They've drawn me ludicrous charts itemising foods I could eat and those I should avoid. They've listed 'good' and 'bad' fruits and vegetables. All that happened after a month of these complicated regimes was that I farted all the time and became incredibly constipated.

Over time I have come to the gradual conclusion that the only way to stay at the right (and by that I mean healthy) weight is to eat three times a day, never miss a meal, and eat as slowly as you possibly can. You can adopt a different eating plan every single week if you want, **BUT THE PLAIN TRUTH OF THE MATTER IS, CRANKY DIETS DON'T WORK.**

They are a total waste of time.

Most women (and plenty of men) feel bombarded with images of a physical perfection they feel they have to emulate. Why? Most of the models in glossy magazines are either teenagers who could never possibly afford or want to wear the expensive clothes fashion editors have put them in for the photographic session. Most models smoke. They do not eat more than one mini-meal a day. They look obscenely skinny and weird in real life. Many famous women who are constantly photographed by the paparazzi spend so much time throwing up after eating a few prawns and a dozen leaves of

SUNDAY

BREAKFAST
Grapefruit
Black coffee

LUNCH
Any appetizer
Any meat
Any vegetable
One-half helping
dessert

DINNER
Scrambled eggs
Sliced tomatoes

MONDAY

BREAKFAST
Grapefruit
Black coffee

LUNCH
Chicken sandwich
on rye toast
(no butter)
Raw tomatoes

DINNER
Stalk of celery
Steak, good-sized helping
Tomato and
endive
salad
on lettuce
(no dressing)
Half grapefruit

TUESDAY

BREAKFAST
Grapefruit
Black coffee

LUNCH
Scrambled eggs
Sliced tomatoes
Apple

DINNER
Broiled halibut
Green salad
Celery and olives
Any vegetable
Sliced oranges

WE

LUNCH
Minute ste
Stewed to

wild rocket that they have developed a thick layer of unattractive fur. They have no body fat left after years of dieting and vomiting, and their metabolism is totally f***ed. Their poor wrecked body is growing the fur in order to try and keep warm. Believe me, I've sat and dined with these women, I've shared a bottle of wine with them at extremely close quarters. This is the horrible truth. FURRY ARMS. A famous footballer's wife has them. A couple of millionairess models have them. So does a stick-thin television presenter. Close up, these women's arms are covered with a thick down – it's the real giveaway of the damage they have done to themselves in order to get into a dress that would fit a normal eight year old. Their heads look too big for their bodies. They have no fat at the back of their shoulders. It is repulsive beyond belief.

The hardest lesson in life to learn is to accept the limitations of your own body. Until I was forty I was extremely thin for my height – just like my mum and dad. I took up jogging in the 1980s but gave it up after I slipped a disc twice. Then I made several television series where I walked extremely long distances, day in and day out. For one I climbed all the mountain ranges in Wales and travelled over 300 miles. The end result: my

hips don't need replacing, but I've had several operations to clean out the joints. I have exercised regularly for the last twenty years, and it is only in the last two years, when I've been plagued with minor injuries in my hips and shoulder, that I've put on weight. I'd like to shift it, but it's not going to be achievable beyond a few pounds because I lead a busy life, and I do not believe in starvation.

PLEASE DO NOT AIM TO REDUCE YOUR WEIGHT BY MORE THAN ONE DRESS SIZE.

Men cannot understand why women want to be as thin as Victoria Beckham. They think she looks ridiculous. Men like women who have curves. They don't even understand our obsession with a flat stomach — historically women never have had flat stomachs without wearing a corset. We will never achieve it by dieting, only by starvation.

Life's too short to spend half an hour every f***ing morning doing sit-ups. Learn how to emphasise the good bits of your body and camouflage the wobbly bits.

The exercises I do are to maintain fitness and flexibility, not gain the body of an Olympic athlete or the stomach of a supermodel. Of course you want to feel energetic, and you want your arms and legs to be toned. But getting rid of a huge roll around your middle is going to be very difficult if it's been there for more than a couple of years. You can aim to shrink it — by regular exercise and eating differently — but you will never eliminate it.

REMEMBER THAT ALL BEAUTY EDITORS ARE IN THE PAY OF THE BUSINESS THEY PROMOTE. THEY GET FREE TRIPS TO PLUG SPAS AND PRETEND THEY WORK MIRACLES. THEY DON'T. THEY TELL YOU ANTI-CELLULITE CREAM MAKES A DIFFERENCE. IT'S UTTER BILGE.

A good body comes from within – it's a mental attitude. You can look great if you're the size of Beth Ditto, complete with total self-confidence, and she'd never get a size-10 frock over one of her knees. If men hate stick women, why do so many of us seek to emulate them? You have to put yourself first, eating in a way that gives you enough energy to get on with your life, fills you up and – most importantly of all – is both rewarding and enjoyable.

Don't demonise food.

You also have to set aside an hour of every day when you'll exercise – and I'll explain how shortly.

YOUR EATING PLAN
ON THE NO-DIET DIET

Plan a whole week's eating before you go shopping. Only buy food once a week. I start every day the same way, by drinking a mug of hot water with a slice of lemon in it. I might even have a couple.

BREAKFAST: Monday to Friday I eat the same breakfast – fruit – a big bowl of strawberries, raspberries, pomegranate seeds, blueberries, chopped-up apples, with a dollop of plain, no-fat yoghurt.

If I am constipated, I mix in a couple of spoonfuls of Dorset Cereals' Super High Fibre Cereal. I drink coffee, no milk, no sugar. In winter I eat porridge – it takes 5 minutes to make and fills me up for hours until lunch. I make it with no salt, no milk, just water, and sprinkle berries on top, not syrup, to sweeten it.

Saturday and Sunday I eat a 'normal' breakfast – a scrambled egg, mushrooms, a bit of bacon. One piece of toast. It's my reward for the rest of the week's breakfasts.

LIFE'S TOO F***ING SHORT TO ABANDON THE GREAT BRITISH BREKKIE.

LUNCH: salad. If I am out I buy one or make my own and carry it to work in a plastic box. I like a piece of cold chicken, salmon or smoked trout, green leaves, a bit of oil and vinegar dressing, no bread. Or I have chickpeas or lentils (drained, out of a can) and chilli dressing. During the day I drink redbush (rooibos) tea – no milk, no sugar.

DINNER: Red meat no more than two or three times a week, white meat such as chicken more often. Game (pheasant, partridge) is great too, and grilled fish (remember oily fish is good for you). I only eat pasta once a week. I eat loads of vegetables, especially cabbage and broccoli, beans and peas. I love green vegetables. I try not to eat too much cheese. I hardly eat butter or cream.

THAT'S IT FOLKS. I'd like to be a stone lighter, but when you get over fifty dieting can make you look much older. If you're too thin you get very wrinkly. I'd rather have a roll of flab around my middle than a load of droopy skin on my neck, and that's the stark choice I've had to make. Also, cooking and eating makes me as happy as having sex – and that's saying something.

Why deny something that gives you pleasure – are you a masochist?

Every day of my life I am told I look great for my age. Truly, it is a question of mental attitude more than anything else. I've been thinner, and I've been miserable. **NEVER ADOPT AN EATING REGIME THAT MAKES YOU FEEL DISPIRITED AND LOW.**

Buying all the food you need for a week in one go can help you to stop bingeing. You can pick at leftovers when you are starving. Build in treats like dark chocolate – but make one bar last a week.

EATING OUT

Don't drink at lunchtime, and order two starters in the evening, instead of a starter and a main course. Never order dessert – you can pick at someone else's portion! Don't have your first drink of the day until 7pm and avoid beer, mixers, spirits and fizzy water. Stick to wine and, if you overdo it, spend a couple of days cutting your daily quota of wine in half. Ban crisps, Twiglets – instead eat a few nuts or seeds or raw vegetables dipped in tahini or houmous. I make the waiter remove the basket of bread from the table, otherwise I would eat it. I try to drink a glass of water for every glass of wine.

RESTRICTING SALT AND SUGAR AND OTHER EVILS

When I did *I'm a Celebrity...*, the reason I took control of the cooking was to regulate portions, make sure everyone got enough to eat, and to make food tasty without using sugar or salt – we were given no seasonings at all.

I used fruit peelings to make tea, turned the outer leaves of vegetables into stock. I didn't miss sugar because I don't eat it anyway. Your body has to be gradually re-educated not to crave these drugs. I stopped when I went on a long trek in the Himalayas twenty years ago. Since then I've drunk my tea and coffee black, without sugar. I stopped eating butter by just spreading a tiny amount of jam on a piece of toast and eating it. I stopped having milk with cereal by mashing ripe fruit into oats and nuts. **IT IS TOUGH AT FIRST, BUT GRADUALLY YOU CAN WEAN YOUR BODY OFF SWEET THINGS.** And eighty to eighty-five per cent cocoa solids dark chocolate is far less sweet than any other kind.

In all of this – be flexible. If I am staying with friends, I don't inflict my regime on them, but adapt it. In hotels, I always pack some fruit in case they have a crap selection on offer. I always take my own cereal. I spend as little time as possible preparing food to eat during the day – but I make sure that I have sorted out a non-fattening, filling lunch and stashed it in a plastic container.

I never buy ready-made sauces. I keep cans of lentils, chickpeas, flageolet beans, borlotti beans – they are all really good sources of fibre. I eat a couple of sticks of celery every day when I get the munchies. My fridge is packed with vegetables and fruit. You have to create your own rewards. But you also have to limit spuds and bread and regard them as occasional treats. Mayonnaise is another occasional extra, not something you are going to drench every salad with.

YOUR DIET AND YOUR PARTNER

If losing weight and getting into shape is tough, it's even tougher when the person you live with isn't interested. The men in my life fall into two categories – the super-slobs and the manically fit. The slobs just ate even more when I got healthy and trim. One husband would slope off to the garage to smoke cigars, pretending he was washing the car. After a massive

Sunday lunch, I thought he had severe indigestion but it turned out to have been a heart attack! Then there was the guitarist boyfriend who ran for an hour every day and would only eat steamed chicken breast with green vegetables in order to look like a stick on stage. He told me this was healthy living – even though he occasionally snorted cocaine and got completely paralytic after four drinks – I suppose that didn't count.... He got me jogging, and after a few months I lost about a stone. But I am completely the wrong build for a runner, and eventually slipped a disc trying to keep up. The moral of this is: just start your plan and don't try to include your partner. LIFE'S TOO SHORT TO STOP YOUR PARTNER CREATING THEIR VERY OWN HEART ATTACK – YOU ARE YOUR MAIN PRIORITY!

When the weight begins to drop off your stomach, I guarantee that they will start to show an interest and probably join in. Men can't stand being ordered to diet. Most heterosexual men think that bread was designed to have butter on it and believe that anyone who opts for skimmed milk is gay. If you work out, and do exercises at home, they are going to studiously ignore you, because (for nine men out of ten) it constitutes threatening behaviour. Just ignore them and get on with it.

WEEKEND WALKING

The best time to build up your exercise is at the weekends. I try to walk for an hour to two hours every Saturday and Sunday. Join the Ramblers and find out about organised walks in your area. Learn how to map read and buy a book of circular walks. Do not be afraid of walking alone, it's a great way of clearing your head and dealing with problems. Walking is the very best exercise there is, and I'm not just writing this because I was President of the Ramblers Association! People who walk have clear skin, bright eyes, and bags of energy. It doesn't have to be a route march. Start with 30 minutes at a regular pace. Build up very gradually. Buy the right gear to keep warm and dry and you'll find you will enjoy walking all year round.

HOW TO SPEND AN HOUR A DAY EXERCISING WITHOUT REALISING IT

Buy some small weights of up to three kilos each – even large Tesco stores sell them now. Buy a cheap exercise bike, secondhand on ebay, or through a small ad in the local paper. Or ask at the local gym to see if they are getting rid of any – often bikes are chucked out when they introduce new equipment. Position the bike in front of the telly or near a radio. Get up half an hour earlier, get your cup of hot water, and cycle while you listen to the radio or watch breakfast telly. Thirty minutes will be gone so quickly you won't believe it. You can do arm curls with the weights at the same time. At lunchtime, leave the office and walk briskly for 15 minutes. When you leave work, walk briskly to the next tube stop or bus stop, extending this distance every week until you're walking an hour a day. Late at night, you can do some simple exercises for your arms with the weights while you watch a bit of telly. You can also do crunches and core body work while watching the box. I do it while listening to *The Archers*! There is no point in pretending you have an hour in one block a day to exercise. You have to split it up like this. I hate going to a gym and joining any classes – it's just another appointment that I may not be able to keep. Life's too short to fill up your diary with stuff you then feel bad about cancelling. Create your own regime that suits you. Remember that every celebrity who says they spend two hours a day working out is lying through their teeth. Don't they have work to do?

FLEXIBILITY

Flexibility exercises can be done at your desk or while watching TV. Choose an armless, upright chair – when you sit on it, your knees should be on the edge and your feet touching the floor. There are various types of stretching, but for ease and safety static stretches are recommended here. Stretch major muscle groups to a position of mild discomfort for 10–30 seconds. Perform these stretches two to three days per week, trying to do four repetitions per muscle group.

Seated stretches

Neck
Turn head towards left arm (as though you're smelling your armpit). Grab the back of your head with your left hand and gently pull it toward your armpit until you feel a mild stretch. Hold for 10–30 seconds, then repeat on the opposite side.

Upper back stretch
Hold your arms in front of your body at shoulder height. Rounding your upper back, reach forward with your arms as far as possible and hold for 10–30 seconds.

Arm cross
Sit sideways on your chair and place your hands behind you on your lower back. Try to hold your left elbow with your right hand and your right elbow with your left hand. If this is too difficult, just leave your hands on your lower back and try to push your elbows together.

Outer thigh
Sit on the edge of the chair and cross your right leg over the left. Rotate your torso toward the right, hold for 10–30 seconds and repeat on the opposite side.

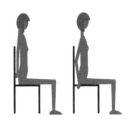

Shoulder back release
Raise your shoulders toward your ears, hold for 10–30 seconds, then release. Squeeze your shoulder blades together at the back, pinching them together for the same period, and release.

Hamstrings
Sit on the edge of the chair. Straighten one leg and bend the opposite. Keeping a straight back and bending from the hip, lean forward until you feel a mild stretch in the straight leg. Hold for 10–30 seconds and repeat with the opposite leg.

Stretches to do in front of the TV

Upper back stretch
Standing up, link your hands together in front of you and try to separate your shoulder blades by pushing your hands together and your arms away from your body.

Chest stretch
Hold your arm at a 90-degree angle to the wall so that your forearm and hand are against the wall. Turn your chest away from the wall to give a mild stretch across the chest. Repeat on the other side.

Torso
Raise your right arm above your head and bend your torso to the left until you feel a mild stretch on the right side of the body. Hold for a count of five and repeat on the opposite side.

Hamstrings
Lean against a wall, placing your feet 60–90cm away from the wall. Bending from the hips and keeping your legs straight, lean forward until you feel a mild stretch at the back of the upper thighs.

Quads
Place your right hand on the wall, bend your right knee and grasp your left foot with your left hand. Tilt your hips forward until you feel a mild stretch at the front of the thigh – you should feel no pain in the knee. Hold for a count of five and repeat with the other leg.

Calves
Put both hands on the wall. Place your right foot about 90cm behind your left foot and push into the wall, keeping the back leg straight, so that you feel a mild stretch at the back of the lower leg. Hold for a count of five and repeat on the other side.

TONING AND STRENGTHENING

Remember muscles don't have brains. They don't care if they are being overloaded with cheap weights from Tesco or the latest Philippe Starck-designed weights, as long as they are placed under some sort of demand. For weight-loss results in the shortest time frame, the exercises need to incorporate more than one muscle group, prompting a cardiovascular response as well as muscular fatigue.

Strength exercises you can do without equipment

Lunges

Start with your legs hip-width apart. Keeping your torso upright, step far enough forward that your front leg is bent at a 90-degree angle to the floor and simultaneously bend your back knee at 90 degrees, without putting it on the floor. Keep your knees over your toes. Hold for a count of two, then push back from the front leg and return to the starting position. Repeat 10–12 times, then rest for 30 seconds and repeat, leading with the other leg.

Squats

For this you can place a chair behind you to sit on, or perform it standing up. Start with your legs hip-width apart. Keeping your torso upright, bend both legs to 90 degrees as if to sit down – do not go further than 90 degrees and take care to keep your knees over your toes. Hold for a count of two, then straighten your legs back to the starting position. Repeat 10–12 times.

Box push-ups

Start in a box position with your hands and knees on the floor. Keeping your torso rigid, bend your arms at 90 degrees to the floor and place your chest between your hands. Straighten your arms back to the starting position and repeat 10–12 times. To increase the intensity, lengthen your legs to a full push-up position.

Bridge

Lie on your back on the floor and bend your legs, keeping your feet on the floor. Lift your bottom away from the floor, pulling your belly button toward your spine and your bottom under. Hold for a count of five and return to the floor. Repeat 10–12 times.

Back extension

Lie face down on the floor. Keeping your feet on the floor and your eyes looking downward, squeeze your bottom and raise your torso. Squeeze your shoulder blades together and hold for a count of five before lowering to the starting position. Repeat 10–12 times.

You can buy all sorts of gadgets and gimmicks to help you, but it's best to keep it simple and be sceptical of machines that promise results in short spaces of time – they make great coat hangers and gather dust really well.

Things that I've found useful to buy:

- Floor mat
- Moderate weights, 1–5kg
- Exercise tubing
- Swiss ball (exercise ball)
- Skipping rope (if you can skip)
- Proper footwear

Household objects that have proved useful:

- Dining room chairs
- Household stairs
- Heavy shopping bags
- Heavy books

- How to shop for food
- Make cooking easy
- Plan meals

LIFE'S TOO F***ING SHORT TO COOK LIKE A TV CHEF

Here's the deal: I love cooking and I love eating, but I'm not going to let food preparation take over my life. I put together food that tastes great, but doesn't look like a f***ing work of art on the plate – it is good, healthy grub. I've fed pop stars, actors, bolshie artists, mad musicians and picky comedians, husbands, lovers and family, and they all agree my dinners and Sunday lunches are the dog's bollocks. So I must be doing something right! Here's how to cook if you're pushed for time, work hard and have no patience.

First of all, let's take a moment to ask ourselves – what on earth has happened to our relationship with food? When did it stop being something we could all enjoy in an effortless way, and start being a way of punishing ourselves? When did we stop eating together? When did we downgrade food into something slightly less interesting than lead-free petrol? Most women now have a very troubled relationship with what they eat. The majority of us claim to be on a diet, routinely banning wheat, dairy, and all sorts of food from our plates – depending on the last magazine article we read, or the last person we spoke to – but why?

Eating is one of the last great simple pleasures left in life.

Go to Italy for your holidays — watch how they eat lunch. You don't get a load of miserable women sitting around saying 'no' to pasta. Italians delight in using seasonal produce, cooked as simply as possible. Women will eat smaller portions, and they certainly don't smear their bread with butter, but they adore vegetables and fish, prepared with confidence that the basic ingredients are so good they need little tarting up.

The British are mentally sick as a nation when it comes to cooking and presenting food. Never has a nation so lacked confidence in its own cuisine. We've got great vegetables, organic meat, plentiful fish — all available at a farmers' market near you. Available on the bloody internet if you can't be arsed to go shopping. But the first thing you have to do if you want to eat like I do — enjoying, not loathing food — is **WEAN YOURSELF OFF THE EVIL DRUG OF SUPERMARKETS.** Do you really want to eat food that has been transported halfway around the country to be over-packaged in polystyrene trays and clingfilm (when Mother Nature has already provided perfectly serviceable natural biodegradeable packaging called skin), and then delivered back to you in fleets of gas-guzzling lorries that clog up our motorways? Do you hate food so much that you will only eat vegetables that have been genetically modified so they resemble perfect little doll's food, serried ranks of weenie sweetcorn, baby asparagus the width of a matchstick and courgettes that wouldn't even fill a mouse?

HOW I HATE MINIATURE VEGETABLES — FOOD FOR PEOPLE WHO HATE FOOD.

We have a crisis about any food that looks a bit knobbly, a bit characterful, to the point that supermarkets now often offer it cheaper. God forbid that we might choose to buy vegetables in a market where they sit covered in earth, unwashed and additive free, naked in all their splendour. One of my favourite places to buy food is the Old Goods Shed in Canterbury, Kent, where stall holders list the names of the farms where the lettuces, potatoes, carrots and turnips come from and state whether they have been

sprayed or not. In London there are excellent markets at Borough near London Bridge, and Marylebone. Wherever you live, you can find the nearest farmers' market easily on the internet.

There's nothing shameful or middle class about caring where your food comes from. You are going to put this stuff in your body, the body you spend hundreds of pounds choosing clothes for and slapping cream on in the hope of staving off old age – so why do you care less about who produced the lettuce and eggs you eat than who made your shoes or your shampoo? Why do people covet John Galliano shoes or a Prada bag, delighting in the exquisite workmanship, the beautiful stitching, the fine attention to detail – but then are prepared to eat an oven-ready pizza that is full of additives, a cacophony of fake tastes, chemicals and processed ingredients? If you care about yourself, then you have to care about food. Simple as that. Change your attitude by going back to basics.

Food, along with sex and relationships, is one of the three most important things in your life.

Life is too short to eat badly, to stuff yourself with s**t, and to cook with no love or care. You owe it to yourself to eat as well as you possibly can.

Don't give me that tired old mantra about 'no time'. I just don't buy that. If you have no time in your life to buy decent food, to recognise that spending time preparing it and making a delicious meal is absolutely the best way of relaxing, then you are truly sad. I care about where my veg and meat come from. I don't have a pet, I don't have kids. So you could say I have liberated time for myself to organise the sourcing of decent food. But that shouldn't be impossible for you too.

JUST PLAN YOUR LIFE SO YOU GET STUFF DELIVERED FROM FARMERS, SUPPLIERS OR BOX SCHEMES YOU CAN SOURCE ON THE INTERNET, OR VISIT A MARKET ONCE A WEEK. USE SUPERMARKETS ONLY FOR CLEANING PRODUCTS. GET YOUR WINE DELIVERED. INVEST IN FILTERS AND STOP BUYING BOTTLED WATER – IT IS AN OBSCENE WASTE OF MONEY AND THE PLASTIC CONTAINERS POLLUTE THE ENVIRONMENT.

IF YOU ARE GOING TO HAVE
PEOPLE ROUND FOR A MEAL,
CHOOSE A DATE A WEEK
AHEAD SO YOU CAN THINK
ABOUT WHAT TO SERVE THEM.
IT MUST NEVER BE
COMPLICATED, PROMISE ME
THAT! FRIENDS
ARE COMING
ROUND TO
ENJOY YOUR
COMPANY AND YOUR
CONVERSATION,
NOT THE BACK
OF YOUR HEAD
AS YOU BEND
OVER THE
BLOODY OVEN
FOR HOURS
ON END.

EATING IN, EATING OUT

A lot of our reluctance to cook at home can be directly traced back to the so-called 'revolution' in eating out of the past decade. Now we eat out more than we eat in. But we generally eat rubbish when we eat out. It's either fast food, lacking in nutrition, full of processed ingredients, fake flavourings, or salt and sugar. We put up with this threadbare level of quality in the name of 'saving time'. Or, when we visit expensive restaurants, quite honestly, generally the stuff we get offered is pathetic. It doesn't matter what food critics say – after all, they've got to keep themselves in work, haven't they? Nine out of ten pubs and restaurants in Britain serve sub-standard food – pre-cooked, frozen, factory-made. And because we so lack confidence in our own culinary abilities, we don't complain.

BECAUSE WE NO LONGER LEARN HOW TO PREPARE FOOD AT SCHOOL, BECAUSE WE BUY COOKERY BOOKS AS SOME KIND OF VISUAL PORN, AND STILL CAN'T COOK, WE PUT UP WITH POOR FOOD DAY IN AND DAY OUT.

We watch countless television programmes about food, and have created a group of much-loved celebrity chefs whose antics we thoroughly enjoy and tune in to watch in our millions, but our level of cooking in our own homes has actually declined over the past twenty years. It's all about a lack of confidence, and the restaurant industry capitalises on our basic insecurities.

In a small Italian seaside resort you go into a café and ask 'what's good today?', and they will tell you about the pasta they have made that morning, the fish they had delivered, the game that got shot by local hunters, the ripe tomatoes or the perfect buffalo mozzarella cheese they picked up from a farmer nearby. What's the equivalent in Britain? The laminated menu listing cod in batter with chips and salad or chicken Kiev? CRIMES AGAINST FOOD. FOR A COUPLE OF YEARS NOT TOO LONG AGO I WAS THE VOGUE RESTAURANT CRITIC AND I NEVER HAD TO MUNCH MY WAY THROUGH SUCH A LOAD OF PRETENTIOUS CRAP IN MY LIFE!

Why do fashion-conscious chefs insist on piling food up on our plates in ludicrous pyramids with chives fanning out of these perilous constructions like edible propellers? Why do they love to serve us food in horrible giant white bowls the size of chamber pots, as if we are inmates in a Dickensian orphanage? How many times have you been in a restaurant,

eagerly awaiting your dinner and been given a melange of ingredients that looks like an edible version of the Sydney Opera House? **THIS IS CUISINE OF THE SICKEST KIND**, and yet critics, TV chefs and most of us humble customers just sit there and pretend that the lukewarm mish-mash in front of us is a ground-breaking culinary masterpiece, when the reality is, it's **CRAP.**

Another of my pet hates about eating out is the horribly pretentious language adopted by restaurateurs who want us to believe that what they are offering is really worth the inflated prices they are charging. In the United Kingdom most of us have our birth certificates written in English, we get married in English, and our funeral ceremonies are conducted in English. But when we go into a restaurant we are confronted with a weird language that bears no relationship to our real world. A kind of Franglais —

as if France was still the place to get the best food in Europe, when it clearly isn't. And in pretentious British restaurants there's a need to tell us the source of every ingredient, generally to justify over-pricing. So, scallops are 'line-caught' or 'ocean-grown'. Tomatoes are 'sun-ripened' and figs 'hand-picked'. It would be easier to write at the bottom one line that says 'all our ingredients are of the highest quality, and organic whenever possible, sourced in the UK if available', but of course that is just too bald a statement. Then there's every chance the menu will contain items that there's not a snowball's chance in hell of you knowing what they are, creating the ideal opportunity for the waiter to be as patronising as possible, shrinking you down to the lowly level where he clearly thinks you belong. I'm talking about things like 'pithiviers' or 'financiers' – biscuits, waffles, crêpes, who gives a f*** what they are? They could be top hats for all we know. Life's too short to put yourself through this ritual humiliation.

PROMISE ME YOU WILL NEVER RETURN TO ANY RESTAURANT THAT INFLICTS PYRAMIDS, MENU TWADDLE OR MYSTERY INGREDIENTS ON YOU, AND MAKE SURE YOU TELL THE OWNER WHY YOU ARE LEAVING.

Three of the few professionals who write as if they love cooking real food, and actually eating it, are Simon Hopkinson, Nigel Slater and Hugh Fearnley-Whittingstall. You'll never see them dish up anything in a f***ing pyramid. They constantly talk about using ingredients that are in season, not tropical fruit and out-of-season peas that have been air-freighted halfway around the world. Eat at Jeremy Lee's Blueprint Café in London and there won't be a pile on your plate, just top ingredients beautifully cooked. Because of the claptrap we put up with when eating out, we make the fateful mistake of thinking that's how we have to cook at home for other people. FORGET IT!

THE JOY OF COOKING

So when you cook, please forget everything you have to go through when eating out. When you are cooking at home, you are in charge, you are creating the agenda. Read a book like Nigel Slater's *The Kitchen Diaries* and you will begin to understand how to cook what is in season, how to use leftovers, how to put together meals that are simple, which rely on a short list of good-quality ingredients.

ONCE YOU HAVE GOOD GREENS, THEN ANY MEAL IS ABOUT A HUNDRED PER CENT SIMPLER.

I have gone back to growing some vegetables, but only in small manageable raised beds about two metres square. I will never go back to keeping a big vegetable garden the size of an allotment like I did decades ago – it ruined my back and all I did was produce gluts, resulting in hours spent making jams and chutneys. I grow a few lettuces, beans, red chard, spinach, radishes, mizuna and rocket, basically because it's really easy and I refuse to eat anything that's been picked miles away, washed in chemicals and stuck in a polythene bag. You can even grow this stuff in window boxes or upended halves of old pipes.

FILL YOUR FRIDGE WITH GOOD INGREDIENTS.

My rule of thumb is to fill the fridge with the best vegetables, fresh herbs and fruit I can afford – that's the starting point for eating well at home – plus tins of pulses and beans – life's certainly too short to start soaking them (the exception is lentils, which you can cook from scratch in half an hour). But I keep a small store cupboard of tins, tubes of harissa, tomato purée, pasta, rice, couscous and bulghur wheat. The only other stuff I buy every week is good yoghurt and free-range eggs. That's it. I only buy meat and fish when I am going to eat it – that way you eat less meat and it's always fresh.

WHAT I COOK

My favourite food when friends are coming round is a really good free-range chicken, *cut down the back bone and spread out, then roasted in a big tin with loads of whole heads of garlic, potatoes cut up in their skins, olive oil and thyme. Or I put the chicken into a large pasta pan with a bunch of herbs, celery, onions and a couple of carrots, cover it with water, bring it slowly to the boil, let it bubble hard for a couple of minutes, then turn off the heat, put a heavy lid on it, cover it with a couple of tea towels to keep the heat in, and leave it for an hour. It will be perfectly poached, and can taste delicious warm or cold. All you have to do then is whiz up some mayo in the blender with good olive oil and fresh eggs — really hard to f*** up if you dribble the oil in slowly. Serve with potatoes you brought to the boil in their skins on the top of the stove and then drained and stuck in the oven in a covered pan for an hour at 150°C. Are you beginning to get the idea? My rule is: very little effort, not a stack of pans all boiling away furiously on the top of the stove. If you don't fancy potatoes, you can cook rice the same way, from boiling point, and let it finish really slowly in the oven, then stir in toasted nuts or raisins.*

Sometimes I make a starter on a large dish (I got a huge tin tray in Ikea for less than £5 which makes a great platter) using different kinds of salad leaves, *arranged by type, another dish of anchovies, and some hard-boiled eggs with chopped flat-leaf parsley. Stick a bottle of olive oil, a jar of mustard and some white balsamic vinegar on the table and let everyone make their own salad.*

I hardly cook on the hob of my cooker at all — I don't want to get a red face and sore arms from hours of stirring. I tend to start things on a high heat and then leave them in a medium—low oven (150°C) until I need them. I'll have a bath, lay the table, play some music, drink a glass of wine. Always remind yourself: eating is enjoyable, not an opportunity to feel inadequate.

Buy **a shoulder of lamb** at the weekend, turn it briefly
in hot oil, just to brown it, then take a couple of pint basins full of chopped onions,
carrots, celery and leeks (whiz them all in the blender to save time) and brown them
in the pan you used for the lamb, adding more oil if you have to. Chuck in thyme or
rosemary, and garlic. Then, take the veg and put in a big roasting tin, bung the meat
on top, season with salt and pepper, pour over half a bottle of white wine, and cover
with two layers of foil. Leave it in the oven at 150°C for at least 4 hours… at some
stage you can bung in some potatoes in another tin, to cook in their skins. Or a pot
of brown rice you brought to the boil first, tightly sealed. Go out, have fun, have
Sunday afternoon sex, read a book, watch a crap DVD. Your food will be ready when
you are. Just stir-fry some spinach for 30 seconds or fast-boil some green beans at the
last minute, and that's it. The meat will fall off the bone, and the sauce will be
fantastic — you can mush up a bit of it in the blender and stir it back in to thicken
it. Why should cooking be any more trouble than that?

Damsons, plums and rhubarb are all
fruits that can be cooked very slowly in the oven and then served with thick yoghurt,
but my favourite dessert is baked figs. Place them in a small oven-proof dish you
rubbed with a bit of butter, just cut a cross on top of each fig, sprinkle with brown
sugar and add a glug of Marsala if you have some, water if not. Cook for 20 minutes
in a hot oven, or around 40 minutes if you're bunging it in the oven that's cooking
the lamb.

I am not one of those people who can only eat fish if it's got the head chopped off —
I love making **fish stew,** but it's a weekend dish as it does take time to
do properly. I make a fish stock from bones and bits, with celery, onions and herbs,
bubbling it for an hour then cooling it and straining it. I generally do it the day
before, but it doesn't matter. For the stew I fry some finely chopped onions with
saffron and garlic, taking care not to let it brown. I add a couple of tins of chopped
tomatoes, the fish stock, some hot paprika or a dab of harissa, and let it bubble away
for 45 minutes. Then I add sliced red potatoes and the starch in them thickens my
soup. Finally, when the potatoes are almost cooked, I add my fish — the thickest bits

I hope this encourages you to take the plunge and

first — chunks of monkfish, gurnard, huss (it's up to you, just reckon on four big chunks per person). They cook in 5 minutes. The stew must only be bubbling slightly as you finally add any shellfish — prawns, clams, mussels — otherwise they will disintegrate. Take the pot off the stove, cover it for 5 minutes, and it's all ready. I serve it with toasted bread, some grated Emmenthal cheese, if I can find it, and a dish of blender-made mayo to which I've added loads of crushed garlic and paprika to make it really hot. When I cooked this on the F-word television show I beat Gordon Ramsay in a blind tasting — he wasn't very pleased! It looks good, and isn't hard to make.

If I want to eat fish and haven't got the time to make a stew, then I just ask the fishmonger what's freshest (I never eat farmed salmon or bass, I'd rather eat something that's had a more interesting life) and then I just stick it in an oiled dish, head on, dribble oil over, cover with foil and bake for up to 30 minutes in a hot oven, depending on how thick the fish is — when you stick a knife in and the flesh comes away from the bone, it's cooked.

I eat **all types of game** — it's free range, low fat, tastes delicious, and never takes more than 45 minutes to cook. Gorgeous white-fleshed partridges, baked in a covered casserole with shredded cabbage and juniper berries. Pheasants, casseroled with celery and thyme. Grouse, roasted for 10 minutes, with brown rice to soak up all the lovely juices. Guinea fowl, split down the backbone, baked on a bed of grapes, dribbled with olive oil. Wild duck, split and painted with marmalade then roasted in a very hot oven for 15 minutes. What's not to love about that lot?

For convenience, I cook up a load of **lentils** and then keep them in a container in the fridge to eat with different things during the week when I'm working. When I go filming, I take a plastic container of my own lunch whenever I can — I only eat a sandwich or sushi when I've got up too late, too hungover to do this! If you stir-fry **spinach, chard or turnip tops** for 30 seconds with some chilli and add them to canned lentils, you've got something delicious. For a **great salad,** mix chopped red onions and parsley into a tin of rinsed canned beans, then dress with top-quality olive oil.

treat cooking as a pleasure rather than a chore.

SATURDAY LUNCH SHOULD BE EFFORTLESS - I HAVE SEVERAL PASTA DISHES WHICH EXPAND TO FILL WHOEVER IS AROUND AND DON'T INTERRUPT THE READING OF THE NEWSPAPERS.

For a quick crab pasta buy fresh crabmeat — one crab shell full does about three people — flat-leafed parsley, a bunch of spring onions and a long red chilli, a couple of fat cloves of garlic, peeled and chopped. Use wholewheat spaghetti — one packet does about six people. Chop up the spring onions — I always do this with kitchen scissors, and use them to roughly snip up the parsley, too, it saves washing up. Also cut up the chilli, chucking out the seeds if you don't want it too hot. Soften the onion, garlic and chilli in a heavy frying pan, add the crab meat, mashing it in, and using all the brown meat as well as the white. Add the parsley and a glass of white wine (any old leftovers will do), plus a generous pinch of cayenne pepper. Leave to stew on a low heat for 5 minutes. Cook the pasta…. At the last minute stir a big tablespoon of cream or crème fraîche into the crab. Drain the pasta and mix it all together in the hot pan you cooked the pasta in, then adjust the seasoning and serve. A meal in 10 minutes. Serve it with a salad made with chicory, frisée, lettuce, red lettuce — the more bitter the leaves the better — topped with some crushed walnuts and loads of olive oil and lemon juice.

Another quick pasta dish: get some punnets of small tomatoes — do not keep them in the fridge — and chuck them in a roasting tin, covering the bottom of it. Strew with sprigs of thyme you have crushed between your fingers to bruise, loads of olive oil, a dollop of balsamic vinegar, a couple of pinches of sugar, black pepper, salt. Roast at 200°C for 20 to 30 minutes, until the tomatoes' skins pop and they start to caramelise. Cook the pasta…. Put the tomatoes in a heavy frying pan and, if they are too liquid, put over a high heat to quickly reduce them to a syrup. Mix the tomatoes with the pasta, adding loads of black pepper, and serve — delicious!

Just have fun. Forget Nigella's cake recipes – we haven't got the face she has to go on top of the massive hips that result from eating teatime treats. We haven't got her willpower to eat only one. Forget Gary Rhodes and his hours of preparation. Forget trying to make intricate sauces and complicated pastries.

Create your own small repertoire.

Eat well.

But above all, make it simple.

LIFE'S TOO F***ING SHORT TO BELIEVE WHAT MEN SAY

- How to understand your partner
- When to fake it
- How to compromise

I adore and value the company of men – God knows I have lived with a whole range of them nearly all my adult life from the age of eighteen, been married four times and had three relationships that have lasted over four years each. I'd call myself a serial monogamist. Or you could say I'm eternally optimistic. Or bonkers. Or you could ask what kind of weird person would want to live with a self-centred workaholic like me, who has a close circle of friends who are pretty similar, who spends a large part of her time in the company of gay men, and who is definitely not interested in family life of any description?

One thing's for sure – there is no chance of me discovering latent lesbian tendencies in later life. I'm one hundred per cent heterosexual, although I know that I'm an easy character to spoof at drag balls! In spite of what's been written about me, I am not at war with men. I do not see the point in routinely trashing the male sex. Men have helped me as close friends, as lovers, and in the workplace. But I do think it takes a lot of thinking to get the best out of them. If only it was just as simple as lining up a great shag!

I have spent all my working life surrounded by men, as I have hacked my way through the media jungle. In my chosen fields, men have been the majority of my managers, although that is changing. When I started out as a journalist in the sixties, I had to learn how to work alongside the opposite sex. I wasn't much better at managing this than I was at sorting out my love life, but I have made progress over the years! This chapter is an attempt to try and pass on what I've found out about co-existing with men as lovers, friends and fellow workers: I invite you to share some of my successes and my disasters – make of them what you will!

CHEMISTRY

Only the other day I was trying on a pair of XL sweat pants in the men's department of a trendy tee shirt shop in Paris, when a middle-aged man sitting on a sofa outside the changing room (waiting for his son) told me that size Medium had looked better as I had a great body. I was incredulous – but there you go. The trick is to accept a compliment gracefully, with a small smile, not anything that will encourage further ridiculous flattery, and not react negatively and treat the man involved as a revolting pervert. Sadly, I fell into the latter category, and whinged to the gorgeous twenty-three-year-old shop assistant at the till about being 'harassed'. Later, the

The first thing to remember is that no matter how self-critical you may be, how loathsome you may find your body, someone out there will always fancy you!

man I was having lunch with pointed out that I had chosen to change in the male area of the shop, and if I found a friendly comment offensive, why didn't I wear a burkha?

A friend once said I was a gay man trapped in a woman's body.

There is an element of truth in that – I certainly don't think or generally act in a particularly feminine way – or what was traditionally regarded as female. Perhaps this 'male' way of thinking started when my father decided to treat me as the son he'd never had, and take me to football matches and speedway racing every week until I was about eleven. I hated dolls, and when I was given one I ripped the arms out of the sockets in a fit of pique. The dismembered object was immediately despatched to the Dolls' Hospital in Fulham Broadway. The following Christmas I was thrilled to unwrap a big box containing a complicated Meccano set, and dad and I set about building a giant crane. Soon afterwards he announced that I had the makings of an engineer – and throughout my time at grammar school dad had high hopes that I would be following in his footsteps. He was delighted when I decided to study architecture, and appalled when I chucked it all in after two years to become a journalist.

At architectural college there were just five or six girls in my year, and nearly a hundred boys. In this male environment I capitalised on my looks by wearing very short skirts at every opportunity. I was a weird mixture of brash self-confidence and extreme insecurity – still true today. I realised straightaway that the majority of heterosexual men never communicate their feelings in any straightforward way, and that many of my fellow male students had left home for the first time and couldn't even boil an egg or make themselves some toast, but they could provide me with correct answers for my college tests in plumbing and structural mechanics.

Most men I've spent my life with certainly never reveal any emotions, unless it is about sport or cars or motorbikes or fishing equipment. I could never understand the nature of any of my sexual relationships – and I certainly forced myself on a lot of men – inviting myself to live with them, deciding I would like to get married or engaged, and easing them into my plans for our relationship, rather than the other

way round. I admit that I, too, am reluctant about revealing the true nature of my feelings – because the more you give away, the weaker your position in any ensuing arguments or disagreements. LIFE'S TOO SHORT TO DISSECT THE NITTY GRITTY OF YOUR LOVE LIFE. Too much knowledge is unnerving and draining. Just accept the raw material you've got – you won't be able to change your partner very much – and not at all if they're over thirty.

MEN AT WORK

It's the same at work – it's almost impossible to change the mentality of men you work with. Better to work around them, recognise their weaknesses, but don't draw attention to their shortcomings. Accept that you are going to have to work fifty per cent harder to get where you want if men are your managers. More women may be getting into middle management, but the pay gap is actually getting wider, not smaller, in some professions. Don't get as irritated, as I regularly do, when the men at work think that some blonde airhead who's just arrived in the office is the greatest thing since sliced bread.

Once you're over forty, you can be witty, intelligent, powerful and hard working, but you will not be the person the middle-aged bloke at the top is interested in.

You will not be the person he wants to have lunch with or pop down the pub with after work to share office gossip. There are some females writing in newspapers I've worked for who routinely churn out mind-numbing f***ing drivel about their latest hairstyle, the length of their fringe, who they shagged last night, or their eco-friendly toilet paper. And they get top billing. They just happen to be attractive, smiley and under thirty-five. I could be bitter, but what's the point? I earn more anyway. The editor thinks they're gorgeous and slaps their picture all over the front page in the pathetic belief that they'll sell more newspapers. No point in giving it a second thought.

At work, men never tell you the truth about what they are really thinking and what their strategies are.

They love congregating in groups, jangling keys in their pockets, discussing the minutiae of a sporting event or the intricacies of a particular car journey. Luckily, normal women are not blessed with the need to indulge in any of this, which frees us up for at least thirty minutes a day for stuff we'd rather be doing like shopping on the internet, or reading magazines. I know this may sound sexist, but everywhere I have worked, men just do this stuff – wittering away to each other like chickens in a coop. It is a mistake to attempt to show any interest or join in – pretending you're one of the chaps will get you nowhere socially (other women at work will loathe you), and certainly won't improve your career.

MEMORY GAPS

Most men have very selective memories. Whether it is at home or in the office, when asked to do something, they often claim that you 'didn't tell them'. Bollocks. **THE MALE BRAIN IS HARD-WIRED SO THEIR MENTAL CIRCUITRY WILL NEVER ACCEPT SOME REQUESTS.**

It might be changing a toilet roll – something the male physique finds almost impossible to do. It might be loading the dishwasher correctly and subsequently switching it on. It might be separating out the washing into the right categories, putting it in the machine and starting the appropriate programme. Men who run big businesses and lead teams of dozens of people, who handle complex issues at work and manage millions of pounds all generally find any of the above as incomprehensible as you or I would find building a space shuttle to Mars. Men will never bother to learn how to operate the timer on your oven, or learn how the central-heating control box works. When it comes to this stuff, those arms (that are so good at issuing orders, or making love to you from time to time) are about as useful as the flippers on a baby seal.

DON'T EVEN ATTEMPT TO ARGUE, JUST ACCEPT THE REALITY THAT WOMEN DO THIS STUFF BETTER. GET EVEN IN OTHER WAYS.

I read once that men and women should set aside time, a special moment when, over a glass of wine or a cup of tea, you chat about the upcoming week, what your individual commitments are and enter them in a diary you keep in the kitchen. HA F°°°ING HA. THIS NEVER WORKS. For two years now I have endeavoured to do this – and every now and then, I tell my partner about holidays, important things we ought to go to together. I carefully write entries in this special diary we keep in a prominent place in the kitchen (just like all my girlfriends do), writing carefully in pencil so that it can be erased and altered – concerts I got tickets for, train schedules, hotel bookings, arrival times at airports. And what happens? If I mention over breakfast on a Sunday what I think might be happening over the next few days, I can absolutely guarantee that within two minutes I'll have a pink-faced cross baby bawling at me across the table 'I never bloody well agreed to that – you never told me we were doing so and so…'.

It's all down to women's superior ability to multi-task and retain instructions and information in our memories at different levels. To get men to do certain things, you may have to remind them ten times – especially if it is one of the tasks I've listed above that they secretly loathe. You can start by writing a list on a Post-it, then sticking it on the back of the front door every single day. They will walk around it. Tunnel vision. Selective input. Whatever you want to call it.

HOME TRUTHS

And let's not even get wound up about the touchy subject of buying food! Men take your shopping list out of the front door, nonchalantly stuffing it in the back pocket of their jeans, and then lose it between home and the supermarket, returning triumphantly several hours later with ten carrier bags crammed full of stuff THEY not YOU thought was needed. You find the list, like a discarded piece of origami, lying on the front seat of the car, unread. It's enough to make you weep – but what's the answer?

> Life's too short to constantly whinge about all the myriad ways men fail at these tasks we want them to do. Don't even try to reshape, train or alter their conduct. Leave it to professionals.

It has been scientifically proved that when women enter supermarkets they shop more quickly and more accurately, they have better spatial memories of where required items are in the store. Don't take over all these tasks yourself in the name of efficiency – are you mad? If you make loads of extra work for yourself, you'll be shattered. Order as much as you can via the internet. Only take your own clothes to the dry cleaners. Only iron what you need for yourself and the kids. Find (or suggest) a cleaner – he can pay for his stuff to be ironed. Or barter – if he does some stuff then you'll do something in return.

Take cooking – some men are good at whisking up a few comfort foods, like making bread, cooking spaghetti bolognese, cauliflower cheese, or putting together steak, salad and chips. Okay, it's not Jamie Oliver or Gordon Ramsay, but surely it's better than doing it yourself?

DON'T SNEER, BUILD ON THIS SMALL BEGINNING.

Let him choose what you are eating one day a week, and then he can buy it and cook it. It's not your problem, and it will hardly f*** up your healthy eating regime once in seven days.

There have been too many times in my life – and I suspect yours – when I've just got on with cooking the supper because no one else was going to do it. Bugger that. Now I eat what I want, buy what I want, cook when I want. It's fit in or f*** off time.

When men come up with that classic phrase 'stop nagging me, I'm going to get around to doing this in my own time' – we all know what the three magic words my own time really mean: this year, next year, sometime, generally never. It's one of the few simple and one hundred per cent guaranteed ways men exercise power and control over women. My best advice in this situation:

JUST FEEL INWARDLY SUPERIOR –
BECAUSE YOU ARE!

As a result of working in television and the print media for many years and issuing complicated instructions to large teams of people, I have developed the unfortunate knack of saying everything I want done three times. The first time, you issue the order, outlining what you want done. The second time, you repeat it, but this time breaking the task down into simple sections so they can't f*** it up. The third time, you go through it all over again, putting in a slightly edited version to hold the bloke's attention and make sure that you are both singing from the same hymn sheet. Believe me, it does generally take this amount of repetition to enact one simple task with the minimum amount of f*** ups, to achieve a result conforming as nearly as possible to your requirements. If this works in newspaper offices, television studios, with film crews and in editing suites, then it will generally work at home. The problem is, trying not to sound like a dictator or world-class nag, both of which I have been accused of in the past (with plenty of justification). From putting out the rubbish to watering the plants to laying the table to sorting the washing, any domestic task will take a minimum of three repeats of an initial order. Any less and you can start celebrating your good fortune!

WHAT MEN SAY AND WHAT THEY MEAN ARE TWO COMPLETELY DIFFERENT THINGS.

There was a best-selling book called *Men Are From Mars, Women Are From Venus* in which the writer argued that men and women use language in very different ways. Women just say what they want, whereas men are far more oblique and circumspect. And because of this, all sorts of misunderstandings and grievances result. The part of the book that really got on my tits was the 'help' issued to women about how to phrase requests to men so that they will rise to the bait and do what you want. It always seemed to involve a piece of flattery or cajoling. Banned were JSP-style orders as in: 'Put the f***ing rubbish out, it's the sixth time I've asked you and the smell is disgusting.' Instead I was supposed to say something like: 'Honey, I know you are really busy watching that television show, but when you have a moment, do you think you could try and put out the rubbish?' Instead of issuing a simple everyday command like: 'Don't forget on your way home to pick up pizza or a Chinese for supper as I am working', you are supposed to turn this request into something resembling a UN peace negotiation by phrasing it thus: 'Sweetheart, I know you've got a really tough day ahead, but I would really appreciate it if on the way home you could…etc.'

HAVE YOU STOPPED LAUGHING YET AT THE SHEER IMPRACTICALITY OF THIS?

You and I both know that life's too short to enter into a lot of gushing verbiage about something as basic as buying supper. Nine times out of ten I guarantee he'll forget no matter what approach you take.

There are many simple solutions that protect your sanity:

* You could get your own dinner.
  * You could cook a big meal earlier in the week and eat left-overs.
* Order a takeaway and text him to collect it.
  * Book food to be delivered – and only buy it for yourself.

Over the years I have learnt to my cost, that

THE MORE YOU APPEAR WILLING TO DOWN TOOLS, STOP THE WORK OR THINGS YOU WANT TO DO, GO INTO THE KITCHEN AND PUT TOGETHER FOOD TO BE ON THE TABLE IN THE EVENING, THE MORE EVERYONE IN THE HOUSEHOLD WILL EXPECT IT.

COOKING MUST BE A PLEASURE, NOT A CHORE.

MEN AND TIME

Obviously men do not operate on the same clock as women, just as they do not speak the same language. When men say the word 'soon' it can mean all sorts of things. 'Soon' home from work is quite different to doing the dishes 'soon'. Basically, 'soon' is whatever they want it to mean – a long time if they're enjoying themselves doing something else, or it could be quite shortly, if they've nothing more interesting on the horizon.

'SOON' is one of the words women are right to treat with utter contempt. Coming from a bloke, it is meaningless.

THE FEMALE CLOCK

Over the years, a subtle form of brainwashing has gone on that reinforces the stereotype that women like gossiping and shopping and are always late. Nonsensical bilge designed to ensure we don't rise above our station. I am only late by other people's agenda, not my own. I don't want to walk into a pub or café or restaurant and sit by myself, so I always arrive a little bit late, maybe five minutes – what's the crime in that? Hardly a flogging offence – my reasoning seems perfectly sensible!

TELLING THE TRUTH IS OVERRATED. Never look for

veracity in every aspect of a relationship – we all lie about everything all the time. Life's too short to conduct a *Midsomer Murders*-style investigation

every day about what your partner has been getting up to and why he is late.

Men lie about where they've been and who they've been with – but what's the point of getting annoyed about it? Be honest, do you really want to have to tell the truth

about what you spend your money on, what your new coat or shoes cost? And I am the first to admit that when it comes to putting out my partial version of the truth, I am an expert – how else could I remain friends with so many of my exes? Take sex, what's the f***ing point in offering an honest evaluation of the f*** you've just had? Why not just let out a satisfied sigh, and masturbate later? I've had great sex, boring sex, drunken sex, dreary sex and inconsequential sex. I'm not a relationship counsellor, but I do know that over the years sex with the same person goes off the boil and other things have to replace it. You can only improve sex marginally, not fundamentally, if your partner is disinterested or lacklustre. Far more important in the long term is a shared sense of humour, kindness and considerate behaviour.

In short, men are not our enemies, but a great resource – but it's harnessing all that, so that our lives are not disrupted to an unacceptable level by trying to accommodate and cater for them, that's the difficult part. Dealing with men successfully can be draining, infuriating and wearing. But it's worth it!

LONDON
DIARY
★
ADDRESS and
1966 ENGAGEMENTS
BOOK

Katharine

I'm a celeb
Nov – Dec 2004

address book

Silvine

MEMO BOOK

TRAVEL JOURNAL

LIFE'S TOO F***ING SHORT TO TALK TO PEOPLE WHO ARE BORING

SKETCH BOOK

JSP 04

schoolmates

- Cull the deadwood
- Workmates are just that
- Accept your friends won't all get on
- And be prepared to hear about YOUR shortcomings

How many friends do you really need? How much of your week do you waste talking to people who bore the arse off you? Let's divide our lives into two categories – the people you have to communicate with in order to work, shop and deal with the practicalities of daily living, and then the people who enhance our lives, give us something we crave, make us laugh, offer us ideas, emotional support or simply a comforting feeling of familiarity.

RULE NUMBER ONE Do not muddle up the people you have to communicate with in category one with real friends. Be careful not to try and please too many people as you go through each and every day – it will be thoroughly draining and you are on a hopeless mission, believe me. When I was appointed editor of a national newspaper, the previous editor was sacked that morning and then I was brought in to address the staff and rally morale. I received an excellent piece of advice, which was: in any work situation, one third of the people you encounter will instinctively loathe you on sight – give up on them and don't waste any energy. Just reduce matters to pleasantries, the bare minimum needed to be courteous. The second third will have decided they like you, and will broadly go along with what you want. Great! But they are not your friends, they are work mates, which is a whole heap of difference. The remaining third are where you put your effort in – you will be able to persuade them to work with you and agree with what you want to do – and as a result you will have a two-thirds majority in the workplace and be able to run it your way, put through your plans and persuade them to sign up to your ideas. This means you only have to put time and effort into wooing one-third of everyone you work with.

RULE NUMBER TWO

Be decisive about how you spend your time at work and outside it. Don't waffle. Cut meetings to the minimum, stick to a list, allot people a short time to say their bit, but make a decision at the end of the time, and stick to it. We don't live in a collective – someone's got to run things from the front – and if it's you, stop worrying about whether people like  you or not, and bloody well get on with it. Apply the same rule to people you talk to outside work, about getting things fixed, shopping, running the shit that's modern living. You don't need to be friends with the plumber or engineer to get something mended. You aren't the greengrocer or butcher's best friend – you're a valued customer. Be civil, keep that friendly banter to an acceptable minimum, otherwise they'll know too much about you. Life's too short!

RULE NUMBER THREE Be very clear about what

real friends are, as opposed to work mates. Friends are the people who don't need to know you – they aren't impressed by you, they are prepared to tell you things that no one else (not even your partner) would have the cheek to tell you. Friends tell you when you look a dog in a dress, when your roots need doing, when your latest shag is a complete embarrassment. Friends are not sycophants – after all, they've got better things to do with their busy lives than sit around sucking up to you.

DON'T EXPECT ALL YOUR FRIENDS TO LIKE EACH OTHER, WANT TO SPEND TIME TOGETHER, FIT TOGETHER IN ONE BIG HAPPY GROUP.

FRIENDS matter,

RULE NUMBER FOUR Make sure that, even though you only see real friends very occasionally, they realise that they mean a lot to you. It might only be sending them a postcard every few months… but don't let your friendship wither to extinction. I have friends who I have known since I went to college over forty years ago. I have friends from every decade of my life, and every relationship. But I can't see them all, all the time. And I understand that they've got friends from every aspect of their lives too and can't fit me in at short notice when I am having a low moment. Friends require patience and tolerance – neither of which I am any good at! At the same time, be realistic about how much time you've got in any one week for friends – don't say you'll do something with them out of guilt because you feel pressurised into it. Make a date further in the future and make it something special that you've put in your diary and cleared time for. I have some friends that I might only see once a year, but because we have known each other so long, we can pick up the conversation as though we last spoke yesterday. I will go and stay with them, or we might spend the weekend together, or we might go out for a meal, or a long walk.

Believe me, I have had four husbands and lived with three men for over four years each, and the one constant thing in my life has been my friends. They matter far more to me in the long term than any of my relatives; in fact my friends are my true family. You have to adopt a different set of rules for dealing with those related to you by blood – and in that I freely admit I have always been completely hopeless. My friends are my peers, and the only people I feel completely relaxed with. When I am old, it will be friends that I spend my time with.

RULE NUMBER FIVE

Don't feel guilty about dumping people when you copy one address book into the next. As you go through life you will naturally make new friends and discard others. You've only got time for a handful of close friends on a regular basis. Accept that you will lose touch with some people, because you've stopped having anything in common.

RUTHLESSLY ANALYSE YOUR ADDRESS BOOK, CHUCK OUT PEOPLE YOU HAVEN'T SEEN FOR TWO YEARS. START A NEW BOOK AND ONLY PUT IN THE PEOPLE YOU REALLY WANT TO SEE.

EDIT OUT:

* The worthies
* The bores
* The dreary school friends who married grey people
* Your mum's next-door neighbour when you were a kid
* Your secretaries from decades ago
* That nice man you once slept with out of pity

DO SERIOUS PRUNING. WE CAN'T LIVE OUT LIVES IN THE PAST – I HATE MEMORY LANE.

WORK MATES change.

Friends that constantly harp on about some golden era when you were both fourteen and who now think that life has treated them badly are a f***ing drag. Friendship is about coping with the present, and looking forward to the future – that way you will always appear youthful, animated, interested. It's fun to reminisce, but in small doses.... I accept that other people will edit me out of their lives too – it's tough, but you have to accept that our lives change and friendships can wane. Don't persist with that insane idea we all grew up with at school – HAVING A BEST FRIEND. It SUCKS. What happens when that 'best friend' gets tired of you, your agenda, your life, your problems? Then you're in deep shit. Best to nurture and sustain a handful of friends... and the group will change gradually over the years.

RULE NUMBER SIX Don't shirk dealing with boring people you don't want to talk to (and realise that sometimes you and I, dear reader, are bloody boring too). Edit over-communication out of your life. Don't waste time conjuring up elaborate excuses for not responding to phone messages. Just don't reply – unless it is to say you're sorry, you're busy, and leave it at that.

Texting is just as bad. Why get repetitive strain injury prolonging a series of dopey jokes in txt spk? My solution is just to switch the phone off. Every week I get a text message from the artist Tracey Emin (who I really like, but who has only one person on her agenda and that is Tracey Emin) telling me to read her column in *The Independent*. She writes one every Friday and then presses the 'send all' button. It drives me MAD, and so I send her a text back saying 'Did you f***ing bother to read my column in *The Independent* yesterday? That's how I earn my living Tracey in case you haven't noticed.' If anyone sends me a round robin email I simply delete them from my list. Ditto emails containing jokes or recommendations about internet sites or blogs.

Life's too f***ing short to log on and read some other sad cow's story about getting up, washing her hair and dealing with a grouchy boss in the office. Delete!!

Blogs are a way of avoiding making friends. You've got all these pals in cyber-space – but so what? They aren't going to come round when you've been dumped, open a bottle of wine and make you laugh. They won't be there for you when you need them.

My true friends have been constant through all my different jobs, my relationships, my houses, my unflattering hairstyles. So what do you do if one of them suddenly embarks on a relationship with a total bore? You have to go with the flow – after all, you will have done the same thing and inflicted a toy boy or a brain-dead moron on them in your time. Try and find ways to meet your mate by themselves – I always say 'let's have a girls night out', or 'let's have a heart to heart' if they are male, and we go for a drink or supper with no partners in tow and have a thoroughly

Jude Deb
me & Anne

fantastic three hours whingeing about relatives, relationships, work, why we are fat, how the stupidest f***ing cow we ever worked with now runs ITV and so on.

Let's be honest – the best nights out are like this – without any partners.

I have a friend who is a newspaper columnist – we have dinner together every couple of months. It is invaluable to her and me.

RULE NUMBER SEVEN
IF YOU PROMISE A FRIEND A NIGHT WHERE THE TWO OF YOU ARE GOING TO HAVE AN INTIMATE CHAT, STICK TO IT.

Never, ever, invite someone else along. Sooner or later, the unfortunate boyfriend or partner will be painlessly shed by your special friend, and you can commiserate. Or, if the partnership lasts a year – you'd better start re-evaluating and see if there's anything about them you can tolerate! Let your girlfriends moan about their husbands and how their sex life is hopeless… but don't fall into the trap of comprehensively trashing men. That's so unattractive, and also, in the long run, not a great strategy – we know men have all sorts of shortcomings and limitations, but if you're not gay, then you have to find a way to work around them and utilise what they CAN do.

Most important of all and RULE NUMBER EIGHT

Try to stay pals with your ex-husbands and boyfriends after you've gone your separate ways. If you loved them so much you shagged them for months or even years, then how come they are now a pile of shit just because you've split up? It's tough on your friends – many of whom will really like your ex – and in fact, might like your ex a whole heap more than they like you! There is only one ex in my life who I can't bear to see again – and as all my friends thought I'd lost my marbles when I married him in Las Vegas, drunk, in the middle of the night, around the time I was fifty, it's no bad thing. Obviously your exes may end up marrying or living with people you find a bit of a drag – but that doesn't mean you can't be civil to each other. I adore my second husband's wife – and I'm a useless godmother to one of their sons. I get on really well with this ex-husband – because I'm not married to him.

RULE NUMBER NINE

Define the limits of friendship. Do not let friends take over your life and boss you into doing things you don't want to do. If they ask you to an event you can't face, just graciously decline, claiming you're doing something else. If they are going to invite you to supper, don't feel you have to cook for them in return if you're too busy. Arrange to meet in a wine bar or cheap diner where you can pay, when you want.

DON'T FEEL GUILTY.

You need time by yourself, but you need time with friends too – make sure you keep a balance.

MAKING NEW FRIENDS

Shared interests is the best route. Evening classes, games, quiz nights, movies, theatre. Sign up for a cookery course, go on holidays where you travel in a group and walk or go to historic sites. Become part of a book club – which is what loads of my girlfriends love doing – and if there isn't one where you work or live, why not start one? When I went to my local theatre I realised that joining the drama group was a really big source of friends for loads of people. You have to remember – you will never be the stupidest or the least talented person there, and you can always make props or help with costumes.

Forget about meeting people at the local pub – too much gossip and no privacy. I go to flea markets, antique fairs and jumble sales, and in the process of collecting have met loads of interesting people. I have become friends with people I've met at museum events, talks and lectures, but the cast-iron way to make friends, in my humble opinion, is through walking.

Join a local walking club, and if the Ramblers in your area seem a bit too elderly, go on their website and check out the groups catering for young people.

For someone who has spent their entire life working in the media, I have made very few close friends through work. I have a huge contact book, plenty of men and women I could call acquaintances – but far fewer true friends.

PLEASE UNDERSTAND – WHEN YOU FINISH WORK EACH DAY YOUR BRAIN NEEDS TO SWITCH OFF.

That's where friends come in – they supply input.

The exception for me was making a television programme called *Network 7* in the mid-1980s – it was such a slog, and we worked every hour of the day in a dilapidated warehouse in London's East End. At the end of a year, a gang of us went on holiday together – all we did was sleep, drink, eat and lie on the sand. We've all gone our separate ways in the media, but still stay in touch. I'll have supper with Sebastian (whose company ended up being my agent), or Sharon (now a top music programme producer) will come and stay with me in Yorkshire. The experience of making that programme, forging a new style of television, brought us very close to each other. But we don't do group reunions – they are horrible beyond belief.

I attended architectural college in London and last year my contemporaries staged a reunion lunch. I walked into the room and thought: 'Who the f*** are all these dreary old men?' Never again! Out of the ninety-five men and five girls I spent my college time with, I see just two on a regular basis – and they are among my dearest friends. Sod the rest!

As for Friends Reunited – meeting up with those girls who made you feel thoroughly inferior at school 'cos you didn't sprout tits when they did is my idea of hell. Those vile bitches called me a 'lezzie' because my teeth stuck out and I wore National Health glasses as thick as milk-bottle bottoms. I was six foot tall and had no chance of snaring a boyfriend to snog at the youth club. They're only going to judge you again if your house is not as swanky as theirs, if you're not married, if you haven't got two kids and a nice car, or doing social work for a living. F*** OFF!

AS FOR THE IDEA OF RE-DISCOVERING SOME BLOKE YOU FANCIED WHEN YOU WERE SIXTEEN–GET REAL!

TIME CAN CHANGE OTHER RELATIONSHIPS IN A POSITIVE WAY, THOUGH.

My younger sister died after a horrible battle with cancer in 2006, and throughout our time growing up together, sharing a bedroom until we were fourteen and twelve, we were not particularly close. Our parents, who had a very troubled relationship, ran the household on a 'divide and rule' basis. Consequently, my father had great ambitions for me – as a young electrician he'd studied at night school and had eventually qualified as an engineer. He wanted me to follow in his footsteps and nagged me constantly about homework and schoolwork. My sister deliberately failed her exams and left school as soon as possible – she felt second best. It was only after both parents had died that my sister and I could become friends. And when she died, I realised just what extraordinary people skills she had. Over sixty mourners packed into the chapel – all paying tribute to her as a special friend. Pat's manner, just like mine, could be brusque. She certainly didn't mince her words, and if you crossed her, you certainly knew it. But, if you were her mate, it was a different story. She loved going on outings with her mates, playing cards at lunchtime, going out for a drink, taking part in quiz teams, putting together coach trips to pop concerts. I miss her very much, but from her death I learned a lot more about how to run my life.

PAT'S DEATH HAS REINFORCED MY PRIORITIES – FRIENDS MUST ALWAYS BE THE BACKBONE OF YOUR LIFE.

Here's something I wrote about friendship in my column in The Independent on Sunday *in 2006 — and it's truer now than ever:*

'Remember when you had real friends and not just the ones on the telly? We might mourn the demise of successful television series like This Life, Sex and the City *and* Friends *— in which groups of thirty-somethings sat on sofas endlessly agonising about life, relationships, and getting laid — but the truth is that those iconic programmes represent a gorgeously seductive fantasy world. The reality for us, the viewers, is that all the demands of our daily lives mean that we have fewer friends now than ever before. Bosom buddies — the people you ask for advice and phone up when you're feeling suicidal, the people you are never going to have to have sex with — will soon be like rare breeds: something to be carefully protected and nurtured. Researchers have uncovered the depressing statistic that the number of people we confide our closest secrets and our intimate problems to has dropped by a third in twenty years. Even more worrying, a quarter of the men and women they spoke to admitted they had absolutely no one they could discuss the really important things in their lives with. How sad is that? We are becoming a nation of lonely, loveless singletons — and with text messaging, emails, speed dating and* *voice-mail, it's so easy to airbrush someone out of your life if they don't live up to expectations, or start proving troublesome. The end result is that we end up not just desperate and dateless, but friendless too. Twenty years ago, people came home from the office and went to clubs. They did evening classes, or signed up for activities with work mates. Now, travelling to work is stressful, and we end up devoting more of our lives to our careers than ever before. We might grab something to eat on the way home, fall into bed, or watch a DVD. The next day, and the next, we repeat the cycle. The success of on-line chatrooms means you can have intimate conversations with complete strangers and adopt any personality you like. No one is judging that midriff bulge, those double chins, your disastrous hair colour or those chewed fingernails. In cyber world, you can be perfect. Real friends hardly exist. Intimacy is a frightening concept to an increasing number of people. The boom in text messaging — more impersonal than a phone call (in which your tone of voice and your mood can be judged and found wanting) — reveals just how disconnected we've become. It's important that we start to rediscover and put the effort into nurturing real friends — time-consuming and irritating as they may be — because, if we don't, we face a bleak and cheerless old age.'*

Back from the jungle and still being blunt

Tough at the top

LIFE'S

TOO

F***ING SHORT

TO SPEND IT

IN THE SAME

DREARY JOB

I've proved them all wrong

- How to write a good CV
- Find work you really enjoy
- How to move up the career ladder

LONDON COUNTY COUNCIL

NAME

SCHOOL

We spend more than half of our lives at work and so that time had better be good.

I have had a fantastic career. Correction: I am still having a great career. I have no intention of retiring, working less, sitting back and letting others take my place. But I've had no children — consequently I've been able to concentrate all my efforts on achieving my goals. Planning a career is almost impossible for so many women — we have to multi-task, work five times f***ing harder than any bloke to crawl up the greasy pole of success in the workplace, and combine all that with sustaining a relationship, keeping a family together, and running a home. It's our right not just to go out to work, but also to maximise our earnings, hold down a challenging and rewarding job, and build a career doing something that we enjoy. I can write that, you can read it, but we both know that the reality is that...

A2

LADY MARGARET SCHOOL

REPORT   Name _Janet Bull._

Term _Autumn 1958_   Form _I7_   Average Age of Form _11.4._

	Marks		
		SCRIPTURE	Good oral work, & usually good homework but Janet must learn with care.
3.		ENGLISH	Really good. Janet works well.
		GEOGRAPHY	Janet works well and with enthusiasm.
		HISTORY	Janet shows enthusiasm i class but her written work is too often spoilt by carelessness
		LATIN	
		FRENCH—WRITTEN	Janet must always give her full attention in class and do her written work carefully.
		ORAL	Her pronunciation is quite good.
		ARITHMETIC	
		ALGEBRA	Janet's work is usually good, but she needs to work more accurately.
		GEOMETRY	
+		SCIENCE	Good. Janet works with enthusiasm.
		ART	Good.
+		~~CRAFT~~ WRITING	Good. Janet's writing is clear and attractive.
+		MUSIC	Janet is working well.
		INSTRUMENTAL MUSIC	Janet has made a very good start.
+		HOUSECRAFT	Good. Janet works very well.
		PHYSICAL EDUCATION	Good. Janet has worked well.
		DANCING	

General Progress and Conduct:-

Janet is always enthusiastic and she must see that this pleasing trait is always allied to accurate work.

Times Absent _—_

Time Late _—_

Next Term _Jan 6._ to _March 25._

Half Term Holiday _Feb. 16 & 17._

Form Mistress _M.B. Jasaroon._

Head Mistress _E.K. Marshall_

Parent's Signature _PWG Bull_

WHAT WE WANT and WHAT WE HAVE TO SETTLE FOR are two

depressingly different things. So let's get back to basics and see if there is any way you can improve your own situation.

I wasn't a complete swot at school – instead I was undisciplined, always in trouble with teachers. But I worked in the public library in the evenings, read a lot, kept lists of films I saw, kept catalogues from all the art exhibitions I'd been to, filed the programmes from plays I'd seen. In other words, I was a relentless self-improver. And it all paid off. School was a f***ing drag. I have always loathed rules of any description and the syllabus in subjects like history was mind-numbingly dull, but at least I passed enough exams to get into college to study to be an architect. And I prepared a portfolio for my entrance examination with drawings and photographs I'd taken of buildings that inspired me. I could talk about my interest in art and literature – by eighteen I knew what I liked and what turned me on creatively.

After a couple of years I realised that college wasn't for me – I would never be as good an architect as my close friend Piers – and so I decided to turn to my other great love, writing. I collected some sample articles I'd worked on, book reviews and opinion pieces that I'd written on spec, and sent them to half a dozen editors (of magazines I enjoyed reading) looking for work. I was lucky enough to land an interview and then a job on a weekly teenage magazine, and within six months had been headhunted and taken on as deputy fashion editor by the *Daily Mail*. Within a year I was a columnist – at twenty-one! That just wouldn't happen today – there are simply too many people chasing too few jobs in the media. Nowadays I tell women to stay on at university for as long as they can, not to waste their time getting a degree in media studies, but to hone their brain by getting to grips with serious stuff like politics, history or English. Degrees in geography are completely pointless if you want to work as a writer or researcher, too.

HOW TO CREATE A CV THAT GETS NOTICED

What will get your job application noticed is not just a well-typed CV, but lists of interests and activities you can add to it. People who spend time doing challenging things show adaptability and dedication that employers will always notice. Extra skills like computer proficiency and languages also play well. And be prepared to take a job working as an assistant to someone you admire in order to get a toehold in an industry or business you want to succeed in. My former PAs have all risen to become drama and comedy producers, run furnishing or decorating companies, or have become full-time writers. If they were smart enough to deal with me, thick-skinned enough to cope with the stress of JSP-style working days, then they can run anything. Some went back to university and took degrees in Arts Business administration so they could run theatres or opera companies.

If you can't take the time to study full-time, why not do a degree at night or on day release? It's never too late to get extra qualifications or to change your career. It doesn't matter if you are fifteen or fifty-eight – you owe it to yourself to keep putting stuff in your brain, otherwise you will turn into a boring, small-minded, elderly person – someone who feels that life has dealt them a short straw, someone who always harps on about the f***ing past. To everyone reading this book I say: it's the future that is the most exciting thing that's ever going to happen to you – not some snog behind the bike sheds when you were fourteen. What you are capable of achieving is limitless, and masses of input from a whole heap of sources and people is what keeps us youthful.

Let's sort out your CV. **FIRST OF ALL, LEAVE OFF YOUR AGE – WHOSE F***ING BUSINESS IS IT ANYWAY?** You're going to be a plus to any organisation no matter how old you are – that has to be your attitude. Discrimination by age is illegal, under EU

Sun Aug 19. Returned from Spain, arrived 9.0 at Perivale. Slept all morning

Mon 20. Went to work - felt lousy

Sat 25 Edd, Joan, & I went up to Fair at Putney

Friday 1st Went to stay with Edd

Sat 2nd Sept Phoned up mum - G.C.E results. I passed both (howzat!) Went to Pauline's party

Sun 3. Sept Came home. Mum & dad gone to Worthing. Joan came round. Went to Lyons club - invented new dance !!!!

Friday 7 Sept Card from Hugo, Finished work, Wrote to Hugo.

Sat 8 Sept Started work in Chemist :- it Not very hard. Went to Roumph's party.

Mon 10 Sept Another card from Hugo! Hadn't posted letter so I just added a bit on the end of it Says he's sending me a matelot shirt

Tuesday 11 Sept Returned to school — (Lousy) back to work now.

legislation, and if you are asked your age at an interview, just ask why they want to know, or if you've not got the bottle to do that, just lie. Who cares? Leave your kids and your divorces off your CV too, that's no concern of your future employers either. Or your current marital status. Instead of listing your paltry qualifications at the top of the page, try enthusing about all your skills instead first. List your interests, your hobbies, how you spend your time outside work. Sound like you'll be a multi-talented asset, not someone who is going to start moaning about how long it takes to get to work each day.

SHOW AN INTEREST IN THE COMPANY YOU WANT TO WORK FOR – and explain why! You'd be amazed how many people came for interviews with me at the BBC who admitted that they had never watched a single programme that my department had made. Why the hell would I ever want them working for me? Out of the door immediately! I am also astonished by how many people say they 'want to meet famous people'. Get real. **I AM HERE TO TELL YOU THAT MOST FAMOUS PEOPLE ARE F°°°ING BORING.** Work is about work, not the remote possibility of shaking hands with Lorraine Kelly or Elton John.

I can spot the good runners and gofers – the lowest of the low – on any programme I ever work on. They will offer to do just that little bit extra every day, unasked, in order to get noticed. Paid a pittance, they are desperate to clamber up on to the next rung of the ladder as a researcher. Good ones don't just get the tea and coffee, they've researched where you're filming, where to get something to eat. They subtly ingratiate themselves by offering to pick up your train tickets. They ask what you're writing about and offer to do some research for you online in their lunch hour. They are the chosen few who will go far, no doubt about it.

Janet Street-Porter

Adrian George

I love CVs of people who've studied history at evening class, worked on archaeology projects in their holidays, put in time at a local radio station or volunteered to help out in a hospital or care home. I am interested in people who perform music, go to concerts, help young people and pass on their skills to others. I am not interested in anyone who lists 'meeting people', 'eating out' or 'travelling'. You've always got to add that extra ingredient to stand out from the crowd.

If the worst comes to the worst, why not just lie about your academic qualifications? They are pretty meaningless anyway. I can't remember if I've got nine or eleven O levels – does it really make one bit of difference? I've got three A levels – but I've met people with five who wouldn't know how to run a chip shop and I've run multi-million pound businesses. My own mother (who was a highly intelligent, if somewhat difficult, woman) lied in order to get a coveted job as a clerical assistant in the civil service. She just said that she'd passed her exams at sixteen, when in fact she'd had to leave school at fourteen and go and work as a domestic servant to a rich family in Manchester, miles from home, because her family were so poor and her father had died, leaving their mother with a large family to bring up. Luckily no one ever bothered to check up on her – and to be honest, in thirty years I have never called up a school to check how many GCSEs a job applicant really had either.

DECIDING WHAT JOB YOU WANT

Don't waste your time and money on these charlatans called life coaches – what a laugh! They call you up, charge you hundreds of pounds to tell you where you're going wrong and why you're depressed.

IT'S COMMON SENSE.

What books do you read? What films do you like?
What telly programmes do you find engrossing?
Do you like meeting other people or are you a loner?
Do you like teamwork?
Could you work from home?

It's not surprising that women, not men, start most of the new businesses in Britain – even though it will mean spending five times

the amount of time working, and definitely involve huge financial risk. Women want to work differently, set their own hours, get away from the rigid hierarchies of male-dominated businesses, which involve time-wasting meetings and an over-emphasis on routine and structures – pyramids of power with middle-aged blokes generally sitting at the top! But before you consider starting your own business, you've got to work for someone else to understand the competition and the market place.

I have been employed by big organisations like the BBC, run large departments, and also spent years working as a freelance, writing from home and working for small television production companies. So I have experience of both ways of working. The most seductive but brain-numbing aspect of work is routine. My motto was never to stick in the same job for more than a couple of years – especially when I started out.

ACCEPT THAT YOU MAY BE FIRED OR MADE REDUNDANT as companies downsize or reassess their priorities. It's not

the end of the f***ing world! Just use it as an opportunity to try something different, and don't spend weeks being depressed and ruminating on the negative aspects of being laid off. It wasn't personal – you have to repeat and repeat and repeat that to yourself over and over again. Every time I have been dumped I have used it to my advantage – I left the *Daily Mail* when it downsized from broadsheet to tabloid format – and had already lined up a job on the *Evening Standard*. I got the boot from Live TV after I made a speech about the M people – male, mediocre, middle-aged, middle class – who run television. Plus there wasn't room for big-headed male chauvinist ex-*Sun* editor Kelvin McKenzie and me in one small new media venture, owned by a newspaper group who had zero experience of broadcasting. I certainly didn't take it personally – in fact I was thoroughly relieved not to have to trek down to Canary Wharf every day and argue why topless darts and rugby (on a channel set up to provide news and gossip) was a bad idea.

I have developed more than one set of skills, so that if there's no work as a television or radio presenter, I can earn money writing newspaper columns or magazine articles. I can deliver speeches, present awards and chair public debates. I never wake up and think my life is boring – I have constructed it so that I never have to do the same thing for too long.

THE MOST IMPORTANT SINGLE QUALITY YOU NEED IS BELIEF IN YOURSELF. Listen: I don't have a university degree, I didn't study Classics, I have never been on a f***ing management course in my life, but I have run departments of 350 people, edited a national newspaper and been a high-powered media executive. In the early part of my career I never did just one job at a time – I worked as a radio presenter in the mornings, and edited a magazine in the afternoons. In my spare time I put together art exhibitions and helped out on new magazines. I wrote for the glossies, for airline magazines and for the trade press.

I never thought I couldn't do something. Be prepared to fail and learn from your failures.

MAXIMISING YOUR
OPPORTUNITIES AT WORK

WHEN YOU START WORK, MAKE SURE YOU GET THERE EARLY. WEAR NON-THREATENING CLOTHES – THIS MAY SOUND AS IF I'M DESERTING THE SISTERHOOD, BUT I CAN'T STAND PEOPLE WHO TURN UP FOR WORK LOOKING AS IF THEY ARE GOING TO A PARTY LATER AND YOU ARE JUST THE BORING PLACE THEY'VE GOT TO SPEND TIME AT BEFOREHAND. FOCUS ON YOUR RESPONSIBILITIES – START EACH DAY WITH A LIST OF WHAT YOU FEEL YOU NEED TO ACHIEVE, AND AIM TO COMPLETE ALMOST ALL OF IT BEFORE YOU LEAVE.

It's important to come across as someone with a sense of humour – you don't want to be considered a misery guts but **DO NOT GET SIDETRACKED.** I loathe office gossip and have never gone out to lunch with anyone I worked with – I can't see the point. If I want a different background at lunchtime, then I take a newspaper and go and sit somewhere quiet, by myself. I do not want to be pals with work mates.

REMEMBER: LIFE'S TOO F***ING SHORT TO SPEND TIME IN A JOB THAT'S NOT WORTHY OF YOU. YOU ARE ON A JOURNEY AND THIS IS JUST ONE STAGE OF IT.

JUST REGARD YOUR CURRENT STATUS AS TEMPORARY, ANOTHER STOPPING POINT ON YOUR ROUTE. READ AN INTELLIGENT NEWSPAPER EVERY DAY, THINK ABOUT POLITICS AND HOW THEY IMPACT ON YOU. DON'T OPT OUT OF LIFE.

Target someone at work you can do better than, and make sure that your bosses notice you by offering to take on all sorts of extra stuff outside your immediate job description. When I went to the BBC as Head of Youth Programmes, I didn't even have an office to start with! I had to spend the first two weeks there camping out in the *Jackanory* library, in the children's department. I spent all my time watching as much BBC TV output as possible and carefully noting who were the wafflers and time wasters at management meetings where each week's programmes were discussed by key executives. The bottom line was that the only way I could build up my department was by taking over airtime run by other people. For me to make programmes, other executives had to have their programmes cancelled – of course they were not going to like it, but did I give a f***? I ruthlessly targeted certain slots, came up with dozens of ideas for every one that was requested from my bosses who ran BBC 1 and BBC 2, and within two years I had 200 people working for me and my department had been expanded to include a whole range of feature programmes, even though a 'Features Department' already existed within the company – I never let that fact hold me back.

> # Get up an hour earlier in summer and use that time to plan your day, to do something you want to do, either exercise, more walking or making a list of priorities.

BE WILLING, BE COMMITTED TO YOUR EMPLOYERS, DON'T EVER SLAG THEM OFF WHILE YOU'RE ON THE PAY ROLL, AND OFFER TO TAKE ON EXTRA STUFF LIKE COMMITTEES AND SO ON. **BECOME NOTICED.**

I was asked to join the so-called 'Equality' Committee when I first joined the BBC – it had been set up to make sure that women and ethnic minorities got promoted. I thought it a complete waste of time and said I was sorry but I regarded signing up to an equality agenda a backward step. In my book I already belonged to the superior sex! I never bothered to get involved in anything specifically to do with women – a complete waste of time. We must not be treated as a special category if we are to compete and succeed in the workplace. Never ask for a favour at work – you'll be singled out as difficult if you do it on a regular basis. When people come and ask you to take on a task,

NEVER SAY THE FOLLOWING:

> I'm already too busy.
> I am not qualified to do that.
> It's not part of my job description.

ALL OF THE ABOVE MARK YOU OUT AS A 'NO' PERSON, WHEN THE WAY TO GET ON AT WORK IS TO BE A 'YES' PERSON, WHO SAYS 'OK, I'LL DO MY BEST'.

If I was a bimbo I would not be running a TV company worth £30m

There is no comeback to that. It is the perfect answer, because even if you fail in some small way, you have at least tried and shown that you are willing. I once had Darryl, a brilliant manager working with me at the BBC, helping to run around £30 million worth of programmes a year. If I ever wanted to develop another project or come up with a costing to pitch for a new series, he never said 'That's not a good idea', but always came up with the reply 'OK, I'll work something out, let's go for it!'

PLAN EACH MONTH, NOT EACH DECADE

I never think about what I am going to be doing in ten years, five years, two years or even next year. I work on the principle that the current job must be what I want to do until a better idea comes into my head. If I plan a project for the future and it doesn't get taken up, I mark out the amount of time I am going to spend trying to get it going – and that won't be more than two months. Then, I file it and move on to something else. You can waste a lot of time and energy flogging ideas that there's no market for. Keep them – you can come back to them later – but move on. If you don't get that job you wanted, try another approach to someone else. It's extremely important to be flexible.

FINALLY:

LIFE'S TOO F***ING SHORT TO LISTEN TO OTHER PEOPLE'S CRITICISMS

Remember you are special. Never let any boss or any other worker try to make you feel otherwise.

IGNORE THEM. If I'd read all the shit that's been said about me, I would have topped myself by now. When I was offered the job of editing *The Independent on Sunday* you would not have believed the crap that other journalists – particularly in papers like *The Daily Telegraph* – wrote about me. Andrew Neil even asked me on the radio why I was qualified for the job! By the way, I had worked as a journalist for thirty years by then, but I hadn't gone through some dreary training scheme, hadn't worked as a news reporter, hadn't spent time working on a local paper. They wanted to imply that I was picked because I was well known! As if a newspaper proprietor is going to put a multi-million pound business in the hands of a halfwit. I had run large teams of people in television for decades. I had produced live programmes that were two hours long, with a news agenda. I had won TV awards – but because I wasn't in their horrible little club, I was obviously crap. I had even presented the same political programme as Andrew for BBC TV for two years, a fact he chose to ignore. The *Telegraph* hatred was more mysterious as I had regularly written for the paper in the past – until I remembered that the man who edited the *IOS* before me – who was sacked – was married to an assistant editor at the *Telegraph*, so she was wreaking some kind of revenge. SAD COW.

MORAL:
rise above your enemies, because you are bound to make plenty as you go through your working life!

← rook shit

I am sitting in Fink River Camp
the bloody birds have already
crapped on my shoulder! So that's
2 lots of good luck in 2 hrs!

You could see the concrete base a
dirt road near our camp site. It's
a 5 hrs drive on dirt roads from
Alice Springs. Two men had dam
the river by making a concrete d..
& a pipe from it supplied the ch..
with water. Now the watershed h..
silted up & the water was much lo..
than the dam, but it was a prett..
impressive piece of work (about
40 ft across & 20 ft deep) all
Lots of birds - olives diamond
done. Now we walked down the
me.. S & the bed west ..
a series of foothills
came to the lagoon

we walk..
..t & bed ..

LIFE'S TOO F***ING SHORT TO WASTE MONEY GOING TO A SPA

- Forget 'therapy holidays'
- Feed your mind
- Hang out with the locals

We go on holidays for all sorts of reasons — and radically changing the way you look should not be one of them. Let's be honest: ninety-nine per cent of us definitely think our stomach is too fat, we don't like the dimply bit at the top of our legs, and we have permanent bags under our eyes that even Touche Eclat can't disguise. We could all do with a bit of 'improvement' — but at what personal cost? When I work, I work f***ing hard, and so the notion of imposing some health routine on my holiday is ludicrous.

SPAS, in my experience, are places you want to **AVOID LIKE THE PLAGUE.** They are full of cash-rich, imagination-poor people being miserable together — you are never going to meet a single interesting person to shag or become mates with in a spa. I have wealthy friends who go to these places to lose weight — to be tortured — or to do a load of work. Sure they might lose five pounds, but within two weeks their weight is back to what it was before. Spas don't work in the long term — you have to change your life for yourself, not rely on some tosser in a white nylon overall who drones on about your chakra while rubbing oil into your hair and messing it up for weeks afterwards.

Ask yourself: what do I want out of a mini-break? You won't get a smaller arse in five days — but you might sleep better and feel more relaxed if you adopt my set of rules and try a different, more realistic approach. My holiday mantra is:

WORK HARD AT HAVING AN ENJOYABLE AND REWARDING BREAK FROM ROUTINE.

That means creating your own agenda — more about that in a minute.

Remember this is the modern world – you are not a monk or a nun. Ignore all the New Age bollocks about rejuvenating your mind – it's just the latest rubbish beauty journalists spout to make us feel insecure and spend money on pointless alternative therapies they got for nothing.

Once, you and I went on something called a 'summer holiday' – then it became year-round 'mini-breaks'. Now, you are considered vulgar and shallow unless you've booked something called a 'retreat' where you pay a lot of money to have what has become known as a 'therapy vacation'. Notice how the word 'holiday' has become a badge of vulgarity. Holidays are what common people do, people who used to go on all-inclusive package deal trips, people who are happy to spend their time prone on a sun-lounger reading paperbacks, slathered in lotion, looking like a pilchard.

The single reason most people use for taking time off work in the twenty-first century is 'stress'. Stress did not exist as a sickness until the 1990s – for the previous decade lower back pain was the single biggest reason used to take time off work. Please understand that providing relaxation and holidays is an industry like any other, and operators have been quick to cash in on what they see as a wonderful opportunity to cater for our new-found 'stress', by coming up with experts who design time off for high-powered men and women who won't feel fulfilled unless they have spent a load of money on a 'therapy holiday'. These new versions of our old friend the normal 'summer holiday' cost thousands of pounds and involve new-fangled experts called life coaches sitting and listening to you whingeing on about what's lacking in your world and then coming up with suggestions about changes in your career or living arrangements.

These 'food for the mind' breaks have been a natural development from the old-style self-improvement holidays where you learned to cook, meditate, went walking, or did art classes – all of which have loads of benefits. But I feel queasy at the idea of someone I have never met before stepping in and re-organising my life.

For God's sake – there are far cheaper and better ways of dealing with a sense of grievance about how your life is shaping up!

Over 200,000 people went on what has become known as a 'wellness' holiday in 2006 — and they are set to become even more popular. You need to have a long, careful think about the fantasy that you are signing up to: a couple of weeks in a ludicrous tropical setting, a house on stilts over water, plinky plunky bells every time you get hot oil dribbled on your 'third eye' by an Ayurvedic masseur in a thatched palm hut. When you return home, there's only one way you're going to feel a week later — thoroughly miserable — when the lapping waves have been replaced by the drone of traffic, and the smell of incense replaced by the pong of your sweaty fellow commuters on the underground.

The big mistake about a 'wellness' or 'therapy' holiday is thinking that it will change your life in the long-term. They are just an expensive bit of Sellotape and don't imagine anything different. Psychotherapists agree that changing your location may make you feel better in the short term, but in the long term it will not have dealt with any underlying things that made you experience a sense of unhappiness or unease in the first place. It's like being in a television reality show — but you are paying a fortune to participate!

At the end of a couple of weeks of massage and chats with therapists you will never see again, you've got to get on a plane, deal with the chaos at the airport and return to the real world of a regular job, irritating kids and partners who don't live up to expectations. And how do you know that the so-called experts you have bared your soul to are any good? The truth is, we are starting to use holidays to deal with our inability to sort out our priorities in life for ourselves, and that is really stupid. If you want to kick-start some changes, like eating differently, exercising, making new friends and perhaps changing your job, a holiday can help by giving you the breathing space you need. But behavioural changes you start on holiday will be very hard to keep up when you return — and you could end up feeling even more dissatisfied than before. A week's 'life-coaching' with a therapist in the Maldives or Bali could cost you well over £3,000. But wouldn't you be

(Guadeloupe)

better off having a different kind of break and setting aside money for regular classes or activities when you get home, something that will have continuity and be an event you will look forward to every week through the dark days of winter?

I have been on every kind of holiday, from a luxurious retreat on a desert island to walking with a guide high up in the Dolomites. I have written about travel for thirty years. I've slept on the floor of public huts for hikers in New Zealand, camped in the Australian desert, danced with natives in a remote part of Papua New Guinea, and I've sailed on the same boat that the Queen chose for a trip around the Western Isles of Scotland. I've slept on king-sized mattresses and on tatami mats in Japan. I've had mud baths, and every kind of massage on every continent, and I've climbed Mount Kilimanjaro, the highest peak in Africa, and in the Himalayas. I've had altitude sickness in Chile and wandered through the Blue Mountains in Jamaica accompanied by a guide called Sweet Pea. You can trust me – I've had some unbelievably shitty experiences along the way, but also some quite unforgettable ones.

But I use every trip as a chance to put something into my head – sod therapy holidays, every journey I make, no matter how small, is something I regard as a plus.

RULE NUMBER ONE Never expect too much from a holiday. It will have good moments, boring ones and unforgettable ones, all mixed up. It won't all be fabulous. I always TAKE A SMALL NOTEBOOK and in it I write my daily diary. It will contain whinges, joys, great meals, snippy remarks about my fellow travellers, comments about the weather, descriptions of sights, plants, birds and number of insect bites sustained! I have kept all my travel diaries going back thirty-five years – and they make hilarious reading when I get back home. They are a way of transferring any of the crossness or discontent I might feel about how the rest of my life is going onto the page, and replacing it with positive experiences to do with the place I am visiting. I cannot emphasise enough how keeping a record of your trip will make it live on afterwards. I have diaries of all the long walks I've done, of weeks seeing churches and eating pasta in Italy, recipes for cake from Grenada, cocktails from New York, great thrift shops in Los Angeles, the names of trees in the forests of Tasmania. I have notebooks stuffed with -postcards, tickets from museums I visited and bus and train timetables.

RULE NUMBER TWO Decide that you will do ONE THING EVERY DAY THAT WILL BE MEMORABLE and put stuff

back into your head. It might be a walk of up to two hours. It might be driving to see a church, a museum or a park that you have never been to before. It might be taking the bus or train to visit another town or village for lunch. IT WILL NOT BE SHOPPING OR LYING DOWN READING A BOOK. Plan to do one thing each day that is input – it doesn't have to take ages. It is not just taking a meal in your hotel. It is not just going for a swim or paying for a manicure. Before you go to bed each night, plan out your next day. Make sure you go on holiday with maps and walking guides. If you don't want to carry heavy volumes, just rip out the chapters that relate to where you are and carry those – guidebooks aren't sacrosanct volumes, like the Bible! It's really important to arrive on your holiday with as much information as possible and to get local walking maps from a tourist information centre or your hotel as soon as you arrive.

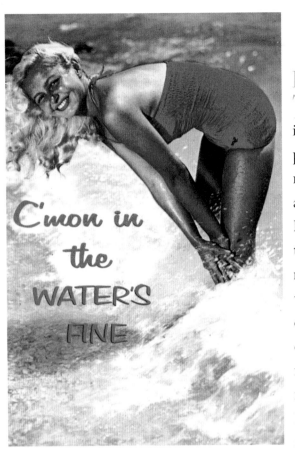

C'mon in the WATER'S FINE

RULE NUMBER THREE

Your companion for this important break is not necessarily the person you have sex with. It is a big mistake to take more than one holiday a year with a partner you live with. Holidays are not shag-fests. Who wants to have sex when the beds are too narrow, the mattresses too hard, the walls too thin, and the air conditioning either freezing or useless? After a couple of days in the sun, you'll be covered in red sore patches and mossie bites, both not exactly conducive to wild sex! Holidays are about switching off, not settling scores. They are not an opportunity to start moaning about your partner's appetite, their fat gut, their inability to put on the right suntan lotion or their refusal to wear the clothes you want. Gay men make perfect holiday companions – they are not interested in your sex life, your fat midriff or your cellulite – they've got the same issues themselves.

If you are going with a girlfriend, choose one who is not competitive in any way. If you like a glass of wine with lunch, then for God's sake don't choose a holiday companion who doesn't drink, or who counts units. Choose someone who likes silence when walking, who will let you read by yourself for hours on end, someone who will give you big chunks of the day to yourself, not some needy individual who feels the need to compulsively fill every hour of the day with mindless gossip or chatter. Don't ever choose anyone in a different fitness league to you – when I want to go for a walk for a couple of hours a day, that's exactly what I am going to do – just a leisurely stroll, not a f***ing route march or speed walking. I am never on holiday to tone my muscles – I have a gym back home for that. Holidays are for toning the mind.

And don't on any account, no matter how much you are tempted, shag anyone you meet while travelling. See how they look back under the cloudy skies of dear old Blighty. And when you return, tanned, refreshed and fit, maybe sex with your partner will be a little more interesting, you never know....

RULE NUMBER FOUR Forget everything fashion editors tell you about what to wear. How much do you want to look like a typical British woman on holiday? No, I thought not. And don't ever believe the crap written about 'minimal' packing. It's not something I've ever been able to achieve. It's a concept dreamt up by stick-thin females who'd look good dressed in a celery wrapper. My only advice is never to waste your money buying new clothes for a holiday – they are only going to get ruined with suntan lotion, insect repellent, pasta sauce and red wine! Or the hotel laundry will shrink them out of all recognition, or press your favourite wrinkly linen frock into a stiff board.

Never buy a new holiday swimsuit before lunch either – go and try one on after you've eaten a couple of sandwiches – at least you know that it will fit in the afternoons. I don't know anyone who's actually ever lost weight on holiday, do you? Holidays, unless you have ignored my previous advice and have perversely opted to be punished in a spa, are for eating great food, drinking every day and indulging yourself. I loathe all wrap-around dresses, wrap skirts, sarongs, and things that tie together. All these garments are bound to come undone in a breeze, and are guaranteed to make the wearer look like a badly packed black pudding or over-stuffed parcel. The 'wrap' concept only works if you have a waist and are size 10 – otherwise, I'm here to tell you, forget it.

What you and I need are clothes that fit around our shoulders and arms, and then gently float away from all body parts below, so that while eating, lounging or strolling we do not look like a series of tyres waiting for their hubcaps to be fitted. For that reason, never buy white trousers, white skirts or white cut-off pants. Take a deep breath and simply leave them on the hanger. White clothes are God's way of telling us we're mutton dressed as lamb, we're embarrassingly past it. White clothes were invented so the *Daily Mail* could print pictures of well-known women on holiday looking like total trollops in their sun wear. Ditto high-heeled glittery sandals festooned with coins, jewels and fringes. Having a lot happening on your feet is never going to detract from your shortcomings elsewhere, and you'll just look like a barmaid searching for a pint to pull.

RULE NUMBER FIVE Please do not opt for a destination that no one you know has ever been to, because you will have no barometer about what it's really like and where is good to stay. The exception is unless you have a particularly good travel agent, or a well-researched up-to-date guidebook.

And if you have bravely decided (as I have on several occasions) to go on a trekking holiday that involves sleeping under canvas,

MAKE SURE YOU ARE PAYING FOR SOME OTHER F***ER TO PUT UP THE TENT AND DO THE COOKING!

I love camping, as long as I am bolstering the local economy by paying for a guide, someone to put up my tent, someone to bring me a bowl of hot water for morning ablutions, and a couple of people to rustle up gorgeous campfire meals in the evening. Don't make the completely false economy of thinking you can do it yourself. Are you mad? Money spent like this is guilt-free. You are employing locals, you are eating their food, and your money is going directly back into the area you are visiting. I hate all-inclusive holidays with a passion. They contribute nothing to the neighbourhood, they are surrounded by high walls and security guards. I will never give one dollar to any of them.

I have hiked all over Europe, New Zealand and Australia, and I love staying in simple family-owned hotels, where they make me picnics, prepare fresh food at night, where the rooms are basic but clean, but the setting is glorious. These are the experiences I remember and cherish, not the night in luxury hotels full of tight-arsed Americans over-dressed for dinner.

Travelling is the best present you can give yourself – and it's better than any drug, believe me.

carnet de VOYAGES

N

E

O

S

1991

AUTOUR DU MONDE
EN 80 PAGES

LOG OF THE JOURNEY continued

Date		Section	N.G.R.	Miles S	Miles C	Times A	Times D	Weather
Sun 24		Marrick Priory	SE 067978	2	108½	11·15		SUNNY!
	✓	Marrick	SE 076982	3	109½	11·45	12·00	and wind f…
	✓	Marske	NZ 105007	5½	112	12:30		lunch by b…
		Whitcliffe Wood	NZ 145014	8½	115	2·30		1–2
	X	Richmond	NZ 171009	10½	117	3·00	9·15	SUNNY
…ANK …OLIDAY MON 25	✓	Colburn	SE 196991	3	120	10·15	10·20	SUNNY
	X	Catterick Bridge	SE 228993	5½	122½	11·10	11·15	
	✓	Bolton-on-Swale	SE 251992	7½	124½	11·50	11·55	CLOUDY
	✓	Rawcar Bridge	SE 299988	11¼	128¼	12:55	1·0	
	✓	Streetlam	SE 310989	12¼	129¼	1·05	1·10	
	✓	Danby Wiske	SE 337986	14	131	1·35	2·45	NICE PU…
	X	Oaktree Hill	SE 361988	16	133	3·20	3·25	getting …
	✓	Long Lane	SE 389998	18¼	135¼	4 10	4.15	CLOUDY
	✓	~~East Harlsey road~~	NZ 418010	20½	137½			
	X	~~A.19 road~~ A19	NZ 442012	22½	139½			
	X	~~Ingleby Cross~~ TONTINE INN	NZ 449007	23	140	6·00	11·30	VERY COL…, GREY.

Date		Section	N.G.R.	Miles S	Miles C	Times A	Times D	Weather
TUES 26		Beacon Hill	SE 460998	2½	142½	12·40		HURRICA…
	✓	Huthwaite Green	NZ 492008	5½	145½		2·00	CHARL…
	✓	Carlton Bank	NZ 522030	8¼	148¼	2·45		
	X	Clay Bank Top	NZ 572033	12¼	152¼	—		
~~TUES 26~~ WED 27		Urra Moor	NZ 595016	2	154¼	12:10		HEAVY R…
		Bloworth Crossing	NZ 616015	3½	155¾	12·40		+ WIND
	✓	Lion Inn, Blakey	SE 679997	9	161¼	1·15	2·30	
	✓	White Cross	NZ 682020	10¾	163			
	✓	Glaisdale (station)	NZ 783056	18¾	171	6·00	~~9·45~~ 10·00	Grey xxx Sunny per…
THURS 28	✓	Egton Bridge	NZ 804052	2	173	10·40	–	
	✓	Grosmont	NZ 829052	3½	174½	11·15	11·40	slipped in ra… sh…
	X	A.169 road	NZ 862047	6	177	12·30		SUNNY!
	✓	Littie Beck	NZ 879049	7¼	178¼	1·00		
		Falling Foss	NZ 888035	8½	179½	1·40	2·30	lunch stop
	~~✓~~	~~May Beck (car park)~~	~~NZ 892024~~	~~9½~~	~~180½~~			clouded over
	✓	B.1416 road	NZ 901041	10¾	181¾	2·55		
	X	Hawsker	NZ 928074	14¾	185¾	4·10		
	X	Robin Hood's Bay	NZ 953049	19	190	5 30		The sun cam… out just as … went paddl…

RULE NUMBER SIX Always explore a city on foot. From Mumbai to Santiago, Venice to Vienna, I always take a really good walking book and explore the city slowly on foot, stopping for drinks and lunch in small local cafés. If necessary take a local guide, and let them get local taxis if necessary. But never take an air-conditioned limo or a coach trip. I like the messiness, the noise and the cacophony of cities, the smells, the colours and the shops. You will experience nothing but a blast of air conditioning in the back of a limo – so be brave. **LIFE'S TOO SHORT NOT TO HANG OUT WITH THE LOCALS.**

Years ago, I created a television series for the BBC called *Rough Guides* – the whole intention was to show you the real version of great destinations of the world, from Senegal to Madrid to Jamaica to Naples. We asked local researchers to tell us the hottest bars, the best small restaurants where they liked to eat, the most amusing clubs and the unmissable shops. The series was a huge hit, shown all around the world, won loads of awards, was much copied, and ran for years. Let those principles guide how you travel in the twenty-first century.

DO WHAT THE LOCALS DO AND YOU WON'T GO FAR WRONG!

LIFE'S TOO F***ING SHORT TO LET SOMEONE TELL YOU HOW TO DESIGN YOUR HOME

- Don't waste money on interior decorators
- Develop your own style
- Change things around frequently

I promise you, you don't need pots of money to realise your personal decorating style – the starting point is a strong belief that if you are happy in your surroundings you will benefit in all sorts of ways. What you categorically don't need is an expert to do any of this. They will charge you well over £50 an hour. Forget it.

YOU DON'T NEED
* an interior decorator
* a big wad of money
* to spend hours poring over colour charts

YOU DO NEED
* to have the guts to define your own style
* to edit your belongings ruthlessly
* to be prepared to spend time realising your dreams

Over the years I have been pilloried, emulated, consulted and paid a lot of money to talk about design. I have lived in one room in a shared flat, a council-owned mansion block, a Georgian sea captain's house on the Thames, a tiny cottage in Yorkshire, and have been through the trials and tribulations of building a brand new architect-designed house in central London.

I AM NEVER HAPPIER THAN WHEN I'M REDECORATING AND THE MINUTE SOMEWHERE IS FINISHED I START ALL OVER AGAIN.

I love shutting the front door and wandering around my space with music blaring out – it's like starring in your own movie without the inconvenience of having a director, cameraman or leading man.

Let's start with the most important room: the one where you sleep. What do you want to look at before you crash out at night? Clutter or simplicity? I look at endless magazine articles about other people's houses – don't they always look so tidy, so organised, so unlike our own? I make sure I have the biggest cupboards or storage I can get, with doors that close completely – forget blinds or curtains. Then I edit my clothes to fit that space, and store everything else in boxes or chuck it away if I haven't worn it for two years.

KEEP IT MOVING
THROUGHOUT MY LIFE I HAVE HAD A TERRIBLE TENDENCY TO COLLECT:

art deco furniture, paper fans from the 1920s, teapots, Susie Cooper and Keith Murray pottery from the 1940s. I went to flea markets weekly for twenty years all over Britain and the Continent. (At one stage I was married to a man who had the same affliction – he'd amassed 1,000 pieces of blue-and-white Staffordshire pottery, 200 bully beef can openers, a collection of swords and military watercolours. Nightmare!)

By the time it got to 1986 I had so much stuff it filled three storage units – where it gathered dust while I built a brand new house. It had to go. I sold my designer clothes from the 1960s–1980s at auction houses and flea markets. I did a load of car boot sales with my sister. I ran a couple of celebrity jumble sales, and sold all the art deco furniture back to dealers.

I purged myself of the need to collect on this scale ever again. The husband went, and so did about seventy-five per cent of my stuff. I kept odd pieces of china, and I display them on an old dresser where nothing matches.

COLLECTING ON THIS SCALE IS A DRUG – DON'T LET IT TAKE OVER YOUR LIFE.

Nowadays, if I see I have got too much stuff building up, too many plates shaped like fish (I collected about a hundred), too many whimsical salt-and-pepper shakers or too much junk jewellery, I pick out my favourite six or seven and get a friend to sell the rest for me on ebay and we split the profit.

Life's too short to think this stuff is going to go up in value – flog it and be grateful for whatever you get.

'EDIT, EDIT, EDIT'

The longer you look at most collectables or ephemera, the more you take them for granted, whether it is paintings, prints, vases, or pebbles you found on a distant beach. Change the objects on your mantelpiece or bookshelves every few months, and you will be surprised how much you'll like the new display. Look at the stuff on your walls and re-hang it every couple of years. Take those crappy posters to a jumble sale.

WHAT'S THE BIG DEAL ABOUT HAVING A WALL FULL OF DUSTY PAPERBACKS?

Do you have so little self-esteem you want visitors to be impressed by your feeble library? Go through every book you own and only keep the ones you loved so much you might read them again, the ones that someone special gave you, the reference books or the ones that are truly beautiful. You can take the rest to a charity shop or a branch of Oxfam specialising in selling books (find one through the internet). Books that just sit doing bugger-all fill up space, which is expensive to rent or buy and could be used more productively.

must be your mantra.

NEVER GET SOMEONE ELSE TO
DESIGN YOUR HOME

Browse through magazines and you'll soon realise you can put together a personal style by ripping off ideas and colour schemes – but not by wasting large sums of money on furniture and curtains. As for getting in a kitchen designer – why bother? You can go to IKEA and pick their brains for free; most stores have kitchen planners now. Most architects (in my experience) are useless at designing kitchens that work properly.

When it comes to structural changes, like taking out walls to open up space, putting in new windows, or building an extension to add light to your kitchen – find a local architect through the RIBA and look at their work to see if it turns you on. Ask if they have a junior member of staff who will come to your home and make suggestions about opening up existing space or using it more efficiently – but pre-set a fee, and don't agree to pay them a percentage of the final costs of any rebuilding. Talk over your ideas, look at their suggestions, and then run the job yourself – it's the only way to cut costs and keep things moving.

I like my surroundings to be a mixture of the old and the new. I loathe interiors that are all of the same period – they date quicker than any dress or coat.

I put pictures of friends in frames I've collected from jumble sales and flea markets or bought new. I change them every year, and keep rearranging them. I collect odd jugs, pots I've picked up on my travels, funny old menus, hand-made walking sticks. I mix the cheap with the rare. I don't let any one kind of object dominate. I found some old embroidered samplers and had them framed, along with drawings collected over the years, masks from around the world.

The key thing to remember when decorating is to keep the overall look as simple as possible.

In London I have a white living room, and to complement this dazzling brightness a metal garden table was sprayed shocking pink to make a great dining table. The chairs are the basic plastic stacking variety, with striped cotton cushions (meant for sun loungers) from a French hypermarket tied on to make them more comfortable. The colour scheme is restricted to bright acid primaries, with a turquoise sofa and homemade cushions covered with jazzy cotton remnants found on a market stall. This look was very cheap to realise, accentuated with weird lights (one made from a cactus which I carried back from the US) and the minimum of clutter. When I get bored with it, the sofa (covered in electric turquoise Bute tweed) will be re-covered or sold at an auction house.

I have had four different sofas in the last eight years. It's important to treat them like fashionable frocks – they are the central feature of the room and you will get bored with them.

I'VE CERTAINLY CHANGED SOFAS AS OFTEN AS I'VE CHANGED MEN. SOFAS ALWAYS ACCOMMODATE MY BIG ARSE WITHOUT ANSWERING BACK. A good sofa is the most important piece of furniture after your bed. A sofa is where you weep when you're lonely, slob out when you're feeling sick, and get down and dirty when you're in that all-too-brief hot stage in a new relationship.

FURNITURE IS THERE TO DO A JOB – **IT'S NOT YOUR BEST FRIEND,** SO WHEN YOU GET FED UP WITH IT, FLOG IT AND MOVE ON.

My style is not easy to pin down. Rubbish and good art are all given equal importance. The main criteria is that my bits and pieces all mean something to me, they are not there to impress anyone else – and that's the best advice I can give you.

HAVE THE GUTS TO PUT YOUR FAVOURITE THINGS AROUND YOU, NOT SOME SOULLESS FABRICATED LOOK DREAMT UP BY AN INTERIORS MAGAZINE.

I don't care if stripped pine is 'in' or 'out'. I buy old chests of drawers or desks and drop sinks into them for my bathrooms – that way I get a set of drawers for makeup and towels underneath. I got rid of curtains in my Yorkshire farmhouse and had wooden folding shutters made. The old pine floors were stripped and waxed, and covered with rag rugs made in the 1950s that I bought in local junk shops. In the corner is a funny little table my dad made from bits of a telegraph pole during the war. I've got an art deco vase full of shocking pink fabric roses from Woolworths adding a splash of colour to a dark space.

A couple of years ago the *Sun* newspaper found out that I had a tiny

house on the sea in Kent. They turned up when I wasn't there and managed to see inside and told their readers that my main decorating crime was painting the walls magnolia!!! The idea that the f***ing *Sun* newspaper is some sort of arbiter of style when it comes to interiors is so funny, isn't it?

Personally, I have always thought that there's nothing wrong with painting your walls cream

— what I can't stand are snobby cows who drone on about how they've chosen really expensive emulsion paints based on National Trust-approved colours, with a tiny hint of blue or yellow in the white, manufactured to an ancient formula by a really expensive company like Farrow and Ball.

Ninety-nine people out of a hundred cannot tell the difference between bog-standard white and designer white paint.

Same with creamy 'linen' curtains. I used scaffolding poles and bought the cheapest unbleached cotton at John Lewis to make curtains for my beach house. The bed was made from railway sleepers by a carpenter friend, and I covered it with old cotton quilts. I buy cheap wool travel rugs when I am driving through the Scottish borders, in blue and white checks and stripes that fit in with my colour scheme. It's not exactly rocket science.

The stacking dining chairs are unpainted galvanised steel, the dining table made from ribbed aluminium.

THE TRICK IS TO LIMIT THE RANGE OF COLOURS AND MATERIALS

– loads of shades of blue, a basic creamy white background, and different grey metals for furniture and lighting. All as simple as possible.

I would not dream of telling you how to decorate, I can only tell you how I do things –

you have to have the guts to realise that there's no right or wrong way to personalise your space – the key thing is to express yourself.

IN BRIEF

* Cut out clutter.
* Choose a colour palette that is appropriate for a light or dark space, one major colour and a complementary one (eg cream and blue for a light space… hot mustard and rich burgundy for a dark one).
* Group your small objects together, and change them.
* Chuck out your furniture or move it around every couple of years.
* Mix old and new, junk shop finds and special things.

LIFE'S TOO F***ING SHORT TO BE A SLAVE TO FASHION

- How to make your body look its best
- Finding bargains
- Putting together your own look

SAY IT AFTER ME: I WILL NEVER BE SEEN DEAD IN

* a poncho
* wedge-heeled shoes
* pvc trousers
* a jumpsuit

NO NO NO!

Personal style has to be something you feel very comfortable with – sod what anyone else says. I have always had a very strong idea of how I wanted to dress. The *Daily Mail* once ran a double-page spread of things I'd worn over the past twenty years – obviously there were some horrific outfits, but at least I looked unmistakeable! In Britain we have the most diverse, creative and imaginative population in the world – look at our fashion, our art, our contemporary music. Celebrate that you are part of this rich mix and express yourself.

WHAT YOU WEAR SHOULD NOT BE A SOURCE OF PAIN, VAST EXPENSE OR MISERY – LIFE'S TOO SHORT FOR ALL OF THAT, AS THIS BOOK KEEPS TELLING YOU. THE MOST IMPORTANT THING IS TO UNDERSTAND WHAT WORKS FOR YOU AND STICK TO IT – SOD WHAT THE FASHIONISTAS DICTATE.

How depressing it is to see women all over the country cramming their feet into revolting wedge shoes because fashion writers have decreed they are the 'latest' look. There is never going to be a right time for certain items of clothing, no matter what these self-appointed gurus might say.

STITCH AND BITCH. From the age of eleven I was obsessed with clothes and learned how to sew my own by adapting patterns so that they became what I thought was stylish – I kept an exercise book in which I detailed everything I made and how much the fabric cost. I saved up for things I really wanted, like a leather jacket, and then rolled it up and slept with it under the mattress for two weeks so that it didn't look embarrassingly new on it's first outing. That was what being a mod meant – it was like a religion. Certain things had to be perfect, like heavy shoes, long, narrow pencil skirts, and handbags lined in suede.

In my twenties I spent four years writing about fashion for the *Daily Mail* and the London *Evening Standard*, attending all the couture and ready-to-wear shows in Paris and London. Never again! That intensive period of being immersed in the lunatic world of high fashion turned me off it – and most revealingly, I discovered:

Many of the people who write about fashion and photograph it have nothing but contempt for ordinary people.

They are not interested in your personal problems – they exist on Planet Fashion, where they truly think that next season's colour or heel height is more important than poverty, mortgage rates or teenage drinking. I used to think all that mania was entertaining – now it just seems obscene and quite irrelevant.

Clothes 1963	cost.	paid for by
5 Jan. Handbag.	1 - 10 - 0	me.
26 Jan. Navy jumper	1 - 10 - 0	25/- me 5/- mum
7 Feb. Coat	10 - 10 - 0	mum & dad
23 Feb. Cardigan	2 - 7 - 6	£2-5 mum 2/6 m
23 Feb. Brooch	Given	by mum.
4. March Blouse	1 - 14 - 11	mum.
30 March Denim Jeans	1 - 10 - 0	£1-5 me 5 mum & d
Scarf	Given	Aunty Eileen.
17 April Shoes	3 - 0 - 0	Mum
5 May Scarf	-	Nain
11 May Nightie	-	Mum
25 May Dress Material	1 - 10 - 0	Me
8 June " "	1 - 5 - 0	Me
22 June Denim Skirt (Brown)	1 - 10 - 0	Me
22 June Tee Shirt	16 - 11	Mum
4 July Pumps/des	17 - 11	10s mum 8s m
11 July Swimsuit	2 - 0 - 0	Mum
13 July Dress Material	1 - 1 - 0	6s mum + me 15s
20 July Bag	1 - 0 - 0	Mum
22 July Slip	10 - 11	Me
20 July Bra	7 - 6	Mum
23 Aug Flat Shoes	2 - 0 - 0	Me
23 Aug Suede Shoes	3 - 0 - 0	Me.

In the twenty-first century the old idea of fashion having seasons is bonkers. You don't chuck out one load of clothes to replace them with a new look any more, but fashion writers still carry on with this antediluvian way of thinking. THE REASON IS THEY WANT US TO CONSUME MORE THAN WE NEED, to keep the business that pays their salaries ticking over. Cheap clothes made in the Third World, often by workers who earn less than their national minimum wage, have flooded into Britain. Now we buy jeans for £10, tee shirts for £2, party dresses for £20, and chuck them out after a couple of wears. They generally look dreadful after they've been washed half a dozen times anyway.

This is a horrible way to dress – you wouldn't eat cheap, nasty muck that was produced in horrible conditions, so why wear it?

The most loyal things (worn over and over again) in my wardrobe are coats. I always laugh when I read fashion editors telling us to forget about coats, jackets are in. Don't they ever wait for a train in December? Don't they ever have to walk to the shops in the wind? Don't they ever have to queue outside a cinema? Unless you have a chauffeur, an unlimited taxi account or a private jet, you'll never ever manage to get through the winter without a thick coat. And don't think that wearing a padded ski jacket looks anything other than sad.

Around thirty years ago, Doug Hayward – the famous tailor who dressed people like Sean Connery and Michael Caine – made me a beautiful long, narrow, single-breasted navy blue cashmere overcoat. I still wear it, proof that a great coat never really stops being useful. I have early Alexander McQueen numbers in brown wool and black cashmere, and beautiful tweed coats by Dries Van Noten that are fifteen years old. I never buy cheap coats. I buy a great coat in a colour or a fabric I haven't already got every couple of seasons. I still have a yellowy green Max and Co silk summer coat from ten years ago and one in bright cobalt-blue suede by Betty Jackson that I picked up in her sale. The only time I chuck out coats is when they fall to pieces, like the turquoise mohair Gucci trench that ended up looking like a matted doormat!

The right clothes should make you feel better – but, for most of us, shopping for something to wear is a horrible experience. Life's too f***ing short to patronise snooty designer boutiques.

A few years back I went into a famous boutique off Bond Street to buy a dress by Alexander McQueen that I'd seen pictured in a magazine. A stick-thin snotty woman approached me and when I said what I was looking for, in a size 14, she gave me a pitying look – as if I had just wet myself – and came out with the following:

'I'M SORRY MADAM WE DON'T SELL THAT SIZE HERE!'

What planet are these cows on? The average woman's dress size in Great Britain is at least a 16 — and by the way, most designer clothes are bought by women over thirty, and the majority of their wealthy clients are not size 8, 10 or 12 and never will be.

The best way to shop to avoid ritual humiliation is on the internet or by using a personal shopper in a good department store. When you buy on the internet, make sure you can change it. Be honest about your size, and ask loads of questions about their cut. But don't ever get addicted to online high fashion — it won't get you a lover, a better job, a nicer home, or a friend. All it gets you is debt!

In-store personal shoppers don't charge any money for their services — I use the excellent team at Liberty in London. They know my size, what I like and don't like — it's always worth spending an hour explaining all this when you first meet. You can ask them to call you when something has come in that might suit you. You can phone or email from wherever you are — and they are trained to solve your immediate problem — the dress for a wedding, the suit for an important interview. They don't force you to spend money you haven't got, they don't bully you, and they know who else has bought the dress you might be interested in. They are experts at working out how to disguise your fat arse, your non-existent waist.

Every executive woman I know uses a personal shopper. They are far more honest than any of your girlfriends.

Don't be intimidated — every good department store now has a personal shopping department and it's there to be used.

Buying clothes this way means you actually spend less, because you pick single pieces that work well and last more than one year, like well-cut trousers or a tailored jacket, and then you can team them with basic tee shirts or skirts from a chain like Gap. I avoid small boutiques like the plague. If you are not a size 8, 10 or 12, they will not have your size in stock. They

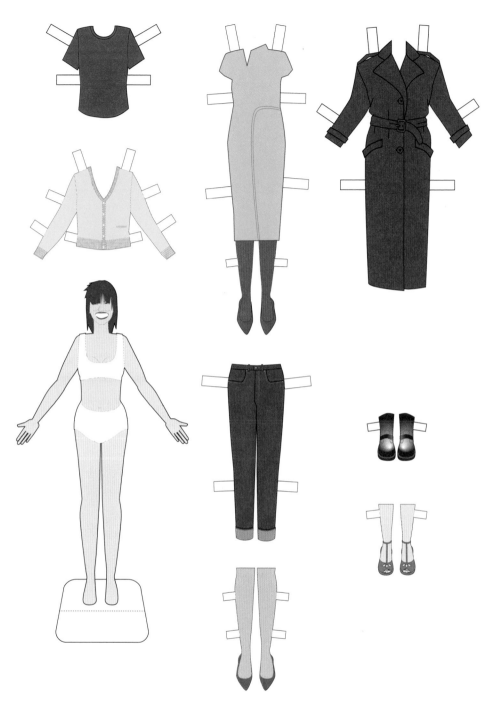

are too intimate, and it's hard not to get swept up into buying things because **the shop assistant is raving about them**. In a department store you can be more clinical and detached.

BUYING JEANS
– ANOTHER ONE OF LIFE'S NIGHTMARE EXPERIENCES.

Jeans are another disaster area – we're offered so many different cuts, high-waisted, low-rise, boot-leg, narrow, flared and wide. I feel anxious every time it's that time of year when I need to buy another pair of jeans. SOLUTION: I simply go into a department store with a large men's department (like Selfridges), select the best-looking young male assistant and tell him to choose me a pair of jeans. I couldn't give a f*** what he thinks about the size of my arse – believe me, there will be plenty of worse fatties coming into this place in the course of any week, simply by the law of averages. Best to select a weekday morning, when the place is virtually empty and the staff are so bored out of their brains they will willingly search through every rack until they come up with your size, in the hope of scoring some commission. Better still, ask your gay male friends if they are chucking out any jeans or contemplating sending any to the charity shop, in which case you can make a charity donation in return for their cast-offs. That way you get a great pair of designer jeans, already worn in, probably from a price range you would never have considered in the first place.

NO ONE IN THE FASHION BUSINESS EVER PAYS THE REAL PRICE FOR ANYTHING.

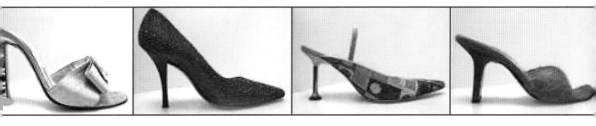

Ignore what fashion magazines decree is this season's look. Instead, try a small version of it, either by choosing a colour, a hot new fabric, a top, or a pair of opaque or patterned tights. My basic wardrobe doesn't change much: men's jeans (longer, narrower), big cardigans in bold colours, white or black tee shirts from Loft (I pick them up when I am in Paris, but they have a website and also sell well-made basics like straight-leg long sweatpants); very few dresses, because they are not adaptable. The ones I do have are in soft jersey prints and do not crease when they are screwed up in my suitcase.

GO FOR CLASSY CLASSICS IF YOU WANT TO WEAR SHOES FOR MORE THAN THREE MONTHS.

I paid over £400 for a knock-out pair of black biker boots by Versace six years ago, and I still wear them every single winter, so that's excellent value for money. I have black suede ankle boots by Tods from the 1980s, Y3 trainers in plum patent that are five years old, jewelled Ferragamo pumps that were a present a decade ago. I only wear flat shoes during the day, but then I am six feet tall and don't need to try and elongate my legs. High heels are strictly for parties.

FIND A GOOD DRESSMAKER

Look in the small ads in your local paper, scour newsagents' noticeboards, ask everyone at work and where you live if they know someone who is good with a sewing machine. A good dressmaker will take your favourite trousers apart, and then remake them in any suitable fabric. Once you've got trousers that fit perfectly, all you need is a couple of pairs of jeans and then you're sorted.

Some dry cleaners have very good people doing alterations – and when you find one, tip them a couple of pounds extra from time to time so that they are willing to alter all your clothes just the way you want them. I have remade skirts from wrap style to zippered, turned them from long to short, made culottes into soft gathered skirts, and bought a Donna Karan suit in a sale with the jacket a size too big and turned it into a perfect autumn outfit for £10.

Ever since I sewed all my own outfits as a teenager, and then made clothes for boutiques when I was a student, I've realised that sewing is not a skill to be sneered at. I have a dressmaker who even made me a fancy dress costume (I went as a runner bean!) for Matt Lucas's wedding last year. She's made me a jacket out of black feathers for a black tie ball, and a black halterneck dress suspended from a jewelled curtain ring. She made little bra tops to go under sheer cotton tops picked up for £5 in India, and baggy linen trousers that are lined so they don't look screwed up.

Buy fabrics when you travel. I bring back lengths of silk, embroidered cotton, plain linen. I buy old curtains in flea markets, pieces of lace. I stockpile fabrics and one day they will be turned into something special by my dressmaker.

A designer dress isn't sacrosanct — it's only a bloody dress, not a religious relic for God's sake. I have had all my designer clothes altered after I've got tired of them — sleeves taken out, skirts shortened, dresses recut. I never bother worrying about what the designer might think — clothes are there to serve me, not vice versa.

OPEN YOUR WARDROBE DOOR. CHUCK AWAY EVERYTHING YOU HAVE NOT WORN FOR TWO YEARS.

* Give it to Macmillan Cancer fundraisers

* Give it to Oxfam

* Give it to your cleaning lady

* Give it to thinner friends

* Or have a swap evening with your friends (crack open a couple of bottles of wine and swap all your unwanted clothes)

Don't hoard the unwearable, the unfashionable and the unspeakable mistakes.

And remember,

Don't get me wrong — I still love reading about fashion after all these years. But I will not be a slave to it. I filter what I am seeing ruthlessly. I decide only to adapt or adopt what is appropriate —

WORKING OUT WHAT SUITS YOU IS THE TOUGHEST CHALLENGE.

Reflect new trends, but don't invest in them heavily. Nothing will age you more than looking like mutton dressed as lamb. Avoid clunky jewellery unless you are six foot tall. Cut out the extra layers, the trailing scarves, the flapping bags, the unnecessary frills. Think streamlined, no matter what the fashion editors say. When you see something that works, buy a couple of them.

FASHION IS EXHILARATING, ENERGISING, FUN – IF YOU MAKE IT WORK FOR YOU.

If you allow it to dominate your life, or be a source of major anxiety, that's not right. When the clocks go back in the autumn, pack all your summer clothes away in a suitcase for the winter — that way you get more wardrobe space. Take them out at Easter, and dispose of what doesn't fit or what looks unappealing!

LESS IS MORE.

LIFE'S TOO F***ING SHORT TO HAVE A SET OF RULES YOU CAN'T LIVE UP TO

* See through the twaddle in the media
* Make your own rules and stick to them
* Stop fretting about finding the best
  beach bag / bath oil / tee shirt

We're supposed to be cash rich and time poor. We have the mental burden of carrying considerable personal debt, some of the largest in Europe. In short, our credit card spending is out of control. We use shopping as a way to make us feel better, but in the long term the inevitable bills end up making us feel worse. But what makes me feel even queasier than a large credit card bill is too much choice. The by-product of our affluence and our emotional and cultural poverty, the logical conclusion of a society in which shopping is now regarded as a legitimate pastime or hobby like fly fishing or judo, is that we are offered miles more choice about every aspect of our lives – as if that's somehow empowering us and reinforcing our individuality. Hey – I can spend a lot of time choosing from 100 different corkscrews, so I must be a highly intelligent, conscientious consumer! Utter garbage!

Too much choice is thoroughly debilitating and solves nothing. It just throws up more problems – the main one of which is that exercising choice eats up valuable time – and for what?

CHOICE DOESN'T NECESSARILY MEAN YOU ARE CHOOSING BETTER QUALITY, OR THAT THE END RESULT WILL ENHANCE YOUR LIFE IN ANY WAY.

Of course, a basic level of choice is a good thing, as it allows us to buy everything from food to gadgets to clothes and even homes based on what we would like to spend and what our personal requirements are. But the level of choice that we are offered routinely by retailers whose only motive is more profit for their shareholders is repulsive. Take tomatoes, for example. You and I are bound to have the same basic criteria when we buy a tomato. We would like it to be ripened in the sun, full of flavour and hopefully not sprayed with chemicals and pesticides. You could apply the same criteria to most fruit and vegetables and perhaps add in the notion of buying stuff grown locally when possible, produce that's in season, stuff that's travelled as few air miles as possible, and is organic, if appropriate.

Much has been written over the last decade about how EU bureaucrats in Brussels have instituted so many rules and regulations that fruit and vegetable growers have abandoned cultivating loads of old varieties of apples, plums, and spuds. Every Sunday, newspapers like the *Telegraph* repeat the same old mantra. Curiously enough, the reverse has now happened, and many organic smallholders grow lots of interesting vegetables, fuelled by middle-class customers looking for something different. Supermarkets have leapt on the bandwagon, with the result that they now offer so many different varieties of tomatoes you feel almost faint with indecision. But the key criterion must always be – are any of these tomatoes delicious? Whether they are the size of marbles or tennis balls, plum shaped or round, hanging on a vine, yellow, maroon, striped green and orange, or blood red, what do they taste like?

Taste must be the primary consideration for buying food, unless you are a complete cretin.

Most supermarkets pack and transport their fresh (and I use that word loosely) produce miles away from the stores where it will be sold, so it is generally not picked at the peak of ripeness — consequently most of it is thoroughly tasteless. And once you have put a tomato, no matter what the variety, in a fridge, you have ruined its wonderful flavour permanently.

Think of happy red tomatoes as friends — they are going to brighten up your meal, so why shut the poor things in a chilly dark white plastic cabinet for the last few days of their life? If God had wanted us to eat tomatoes that lived in fridges he wouldn't have created them growing from yellow flowers on large green leafy plants that thrive on just two things — water and hot sun — neither of which is found inside a refrigerator.

I used to love the smell of my grandfather's house in Southgate, North London, where he grew all his own vegetables and kept chickens and ducks in the back garden. The sideboard was packed with red and green and orange stripy tomatoes ripening in large bowls, marrows sat in wooden boxes on the kitchen floor and there were jars of chutney under the stairs along with ranks of bottled plums and damsons ready for the winter. The smell was overpowering, heavy and seductive. The smell of summer. Not one encountered in the aisles of our supermarkets.

And it's not just major supermarket chains who are guilty of giving us meaningless choice. Take Whole Foods, who specialise in organic food. They dominate the American market and have built up a billion-dollar empire with the patronage of the health-conscious middle class in major cities across the USA. Now they seek to do the same in Britain, opening a massive flagship shop of 7,500 square metres on Kensington High Street, in the middle of the richest borough in Britain, a department store for the most discerning foodie. They offer shoppers a hundred kinds of olive oil, forty different kinds of breads, forty types of sausages, seventeen kinds of coffee beans, and over four hundred cheeses. Harrods with a conscience, if you like. Banks of cabbages and lettuces, sprayed to look ultra-fresh and glistening – the way you certainly won't be feeling after spending hours wandering up and down the aisles trying to decide what to buy. Twenty-one different kinds of tomato! Less than forty per cent of the produce is organic, and it is sourced from all over the world, offering us what appears to be

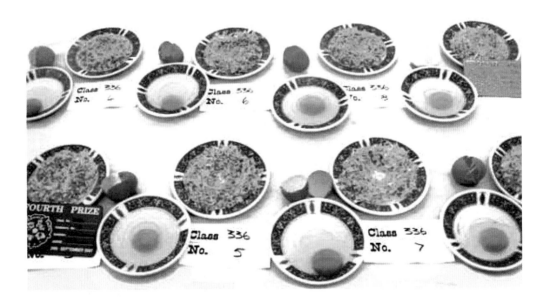

LIFE'S TOO SHORT FOR

the pinnacle of choice – but what does that really mean? I'll tell you – it represents the death of the small retailer, the kind of place where an owner imposes their personal taste on the contents of the store and customers buy that knowledge.

I'd rather visit a shop where I am offered a couple of kinds of coffee, tasted and chosen by the person behind the counter. I want to buy bread that they have sourced, that they like eating. There's a little delicatessen on the main street in Whitstable, Kent, that does just that. It's tiny, only holds about three people, but the owners have chosen the cheese, they've sourced the olives. They have selected a few wines that complement their wares. They have wild boar pâté, delicious Spanish ham. Anything from this shop makes the basis of an instantly delicious supper. Sometimes there are baskets of vine tomatoes or slabs of focaccia, strewn with sea salt and rosemary. This is a shop where the owners eat what they sell. In towns and large villages in France, Italy and Spain, these shops and stalls in weekly markets still exist.

Choice is a complete waste of time when it comes to food, unless that choice has been made by someone with impressive taste and a commitment to quality

– not an executive in a food chain whose primary concern is meeting quotas and dealing with marketing initiatives coming from central office, which could be hundreds of miles away. All over Britain small shops are

THAT KIND OF CHOICE.

struggling as we sign up to this mad notion of choice, opting to buy our food in vast supermarkets where convenience overrules any other consideration. And the irony is, we end up spending more money on food we won't eat, and buying stuff we don't need and won't use simply because it was offered to us.

Marks and Spencer is another case in point – how many bloody types of bread do they sell? It doesn't matter what they call it, M and S bread will never measure up to that produced by Betty's bakery in Yorkshire, where a Fitness loaf is packed full of nutritious seeds and feels chunky and heavy like an old-fashioned loaf, not a substitute for a bath sponge. The reason why people form a queue every day outside branches of Betty's in York, Harrogate, Northallerton and Ilkley is because they know that the bread they are going to purchase is made by experts. It tastes like bread.

Choice is exhausting and a vastly over-rated concept, and no more so than when you go into a clothes shop in search of what we might consider basic clothing.

Once you could buy a plain white tee shirt in Gap, with a round neck or V neck, with or without a pocket. It was a staple in many a holiday wardrobe, chucked away after a couple of years when it had gone grey or blue because you stuck it in the machine with jeans by mistake. Then, Gap decided to enthusiastically embrace the concept of 'choice'. Now we have stretchy tee shirts that cling to our bulging midriffs, we have thin tee shirts that we are

supposed to buy several of in different colours and 'layer' – which for most women simply means drawing attention to the rolls of cellulite around your waist. Believe me, layering, like wrap dresses, is a concept best left to those under twenty. After that you look like a parcel that's coming undone or a war victim dressed by a relief agency.

WHEN YOU FIND A TEE SHIRT THAT WORKS, BUY TEN. SAME FOR SIMPLE COTTON UNDERWEAR. IT CUTS OUT HOURS OF SHOPPING OVER THE COMING YEAR.

When my old pants and tee shirts go grey, I use them as dusters or cloths to wash the car. I am not being miserly, just recycling.

THE BEST OF ANYTHING IS A RUBBISH CONCEPT

Every week, newspapers and colour magazines fill their pages with lists of 'the best' gadgets, sofas, lampshades, compost makers, beach bags and solar-powered lighting. I flick through these articles and tear them out. But do I ever buy anything? Never. I worry about the taste of the journalists who wrote the piece. I worry that they made their choice based on a press release or an important advertiser or a freebie. Unless I know them personally, I simply don't believe what they say, and neither should you. All of it is simply geared to getting us to consume more – and that is surely a bad thing.

Life should be getting simpler, not more complicated, as we sift our way through these choices we never realised we had to make. How can there really be one mixing bowl that's better than another, one purse that's the 'best' choice or one set of tea towels that ticks all the right boxes? Get real – choice is a drug you have to kick.

LIFE'S TOO SHORT TO WASTE ENERGY ON THESE UNIMPORTANT SELECTIONS OF THINGS WE DON'T REALLY NEED.

Real choice can only be achieved by setting your priorities and sticking to them, from choosing a car to buying food, clothes, even a home. Don't be afraid to chuck out the notion of valuing choice – it doesn't mean you are behind the times, stuck in your ways, narrow minded, penny pinching or thrifty. IT MEANS YOU ARE SUPER SMART. It's tough, and many people might sneer, but by eliminating excess choice, you immediately feel liberated from much of the dross of modern life. Stick to local shops, or the recommendations of people you know.

ONLY BUY WHAT YOU NEED, FROM PEOPLE WHO HAVE SAMPLED OR USED WHAT YOU ARE BUYING.

Go on your instinct, not the wordy crap of some office junior on a glossy magazine or a work-experience person on a newspaper filling a space on a features page where an ad got cancelled.

HOW CAN THERE BE A 'BEST' BATH OIL? USE YOUR HEAD.

RULES, RULES, RULES

Along with a plethora of unnecessary choice, we are constantly being assaulted with 'rules' to live our lives by, from what to eat, to how to shop, to ethical living. In this book I am begging you to set your own agenda, not to be dictated to by outside interests whose only concern is profits, not quality of life. This book isn't a manual with an agenda you can cut out and keep, a list of rules that will help organise and reshape your life and improve it in some unspecified mysterious way. No way! Once we left school, I hoped we left the concept of rules behind. I am a person who has always loathed any figure of authority, rules of any kind, from my brief period in the Girl Guides, to my short-lived time as a monitor (never a prefect) at secondary school, to my stint as a shop assistant in Woolworths and my hopeless couple of months as a trainee clerical officer in the civil service.

I HATE RULES UNLESS THEY ARE OF MY OWN MAKING.

Every day we seem to be targeted by so-called 'experts' telling us how to conduct our lives, and the most irritating are employed by the ultimate in nanny states, the British Government. We have Health and Safety notices on footpaths, large ugly signs banning smoking in the porches of beautiful medieval churches. Walk by a river and there's a stupid sign telling you the water is cold – no, really?? We have directives telling us to eat five portions of fruit and vegetables a day for our well-being, and guidelines from the Department of Health stating that women should not drink more than fourteen units of alcohol a week and men twenty-one. None of these so-called 'initiatives' has done a single thing to stop young people drinking and smoking too much, or the collective weight of the nation verging on that of a million jumbo jets. Time and again, rules dictated from afar don't work.

I care about global warming as much as the next person, but 'ethical living' is monitored by rule-making busy bodies.

First we were told to fly less, use the train more, to carbon-offset all our travel. Then we were told that tree planting is not the solution as trees can trap the wrong gasses, and then it turned out that some of the companies set up to run all these carbon-offsetting schemes were investing in schemes that would never really make much impact. Confused? I certainly am. Remember when we were told plastic bags were eco-disasters, and one after another major stores said they would stop handing them out or charge for them. Then Sainsbury's had the 'bright' idea of commissioning fashionable designer Anya Hindmarch to come up with a £5 canvas shopper, on the side of which was emblazoned the motto 'Not a plastic bag'. It sold out straightaway and then started to change hands on the internet for up to £45! Then we discovered that Anya's bags had been made in factories in China where wages and working conditions left a great deal to be desired. So these so-called 'ethical bags' turned out to have been made by poor workers in a country halfway around the world that's one of the planet's major polluters. No wonder people question every day if it's worth making a personal effort to live their lives by green values, when so many businessmen are plainly exploiting the current focus on the environment by producing goods that (on the surface) seem to tick all the right boxes.

I look at a factory spewing out fumes in China, Russia, Eastern Europe or Korea and then I walk down to the recycling bins clutching my re-useable canvas bags full of newspapers, bottles and tins, and wonder if I am really making any difference whatsoever, especially when there are plenty of arguments about the value of recycling. I take care to buy recycled toilet rolls and kitchen towels, but is using paper hankies a crime? If the hard-core eco-lobby had their way we'd all be using earth toilets, torn up old bits of newspaper, making compost with our food scraps and installing wind turbines on the roof. But wind turbines aren't a solution on an individual scale – you can't store the electricity, and they can be an eyesore. Why not just use less power? And the massive wind farms being built off the coast around Britain have another problem no one in government wants to talk much about, and that is the building and location of the large processing plants for this power when it is brought onshore, often in remote coastal areas of outstanding natural beauty. To me, these reprocessing units are as repellent as nuclear power stations – and government ministers will make sure that any planning considerations or local objections will be overruled, all in the name of green energy.

DECIDING HOW TO LIVE IN AN ENVIRONMENTALLY FRIENDLY FASHION THROWS UP MORE QUESTIONS THAN IT EVER ANSWERS.

You could spend hours debating whether buying beans flown in from Kenya is a good or a bad thing. On the one hand, it's a lot of air miles, so bad for the ozone layer, and the beans won't exactly be fresh by the time they reach you, but on the other hand, your pounds are helping poor rural families get educated and have food.

EVERY DAY, ONE SET OF RULES IS SUPERSEDED BY ANOTHER. NO WONDER WE ARE CONFUSED.

Remember when butter was bad for you, and low-fat spreads were all the rage? Then we were told light, easy-to-spread substitutes couldn't lower your cholesterol by themselves, and good old butter was back in fashion. Finally, the Mediterranean diet, with plenty of olive oil instead of butter, simply grilled fish, fresh vegetables and red wine, was touted as the way to a longer life and less heart disease. Living the Mediterranean diet only works in the Mediterranean, where it has evolved by using seasonal, local ingredients. It's pretty potty to try and emulate this in Fife in December or Yorkshire in March.

Rules are invented by public relations and marketing people anxious to promote their wares.

Ninety per cent of all the so-called 'scientific evidence' you read in the papers or hear about on radio and television comes from surveys that have been funded by special-interest groups – fruit growers who want you to eat more blueberries, vegetable farmers keen to flog cabbage and broccoli. Even doctors regularly prescribe painkillers and other drugs simply because they've been pestered by salesmen and ads in the medical journals. We're told that sprouts cure cancer, raspberries help your heart, broccoli is a super food and oily fish makes you brainier. All comical if it were not for the fact that so many of us avidly read and believe these dodgy findings. There's a charity called Sense About Science (www.senseaboutscience.org.uk) – checking out their reports, which are written by independent scientists and health professionals (who are not funded by corporate business), via their website is one way of stripping out the mumbo jumbo that passes for scientific fact in our daily lives.

THE 'RULES' WITHIN THIS BOOK ARE SUGGESTIONS FOR WAYS YOU CAN SIMPLIFY YOUR LIFE - GOALS FOR YOU TO SET FOR YOURSELF, NOT EDICTS TO BE OBEYED AND SOD THE CONSEQUENCES.

Deciding how much time you are prepared to devote to shopping ethically, recycling and running your home in an environmentally aware way is purely a matter for you alone.

THE MAIN THING TO REMEMBER IS NOT TO BE BULLIED, ESPECIALLY BY PEOPLE WHO ULTIMATELY ARE ONLY INTERESTED IN GETTING YOUR MONEY FIRST, AND SAVING THE PLANET SECOND.

MAKE YOUR OWN RULES - AND CHANGE THEM WHEN IT SUITS YOU.

We're not monks and nuns living in the Middle Ages – our lives must be enjoyable and contain pleasure as well as work. Be clear about which ethical values and consumer choices make you feel comfortable – and you shouldn't feel guilty as a result.

FINALLY...

This book was written to make you feel good about yourself. Life should not be a series of tests which you fail to varying degrees, but a chance to celebrate your individuality. Above all, have a laugh...and thank God you don't have to live up to some ridiculous notion of perfection. Take a look at celebrities like Victoria Beckham – do they really look happy?

Life's too f***ing short to be on a permanent diet, worried about whether your clothes have been approved by the style police, and whether you're clutching the latest bag.

TAKE CHARGE OF YOUR AGENDA AND CUT OUT THE CRAP. GOOD LUCK.

IN MEMORY OF DAINTON

Thanks to Peter, Neil, Emma and all my long-suffering friends.

LONDON BOROUGH OF WANDSWORTH	
501307251	
Askews	24-Jan-2008
158.1 STRE	£12.99
	WWX0002707/0255

First published in 2008 by
Quadrille Publishing Limited
Alhambra House
27–31 Charing Cross Road
London WC2H OLS

Editorial Director: Anne Furniss
Creative Director: Helen Lewis
Editor: Jenni Muir
Picture Research/Digital Work: Paul Babb
Original Pictures: Paul and Anne Babb, Janet Street-Porter
Exercise/paper doll illustrations: Bridget Bodoano
Exercises: Jonathan Parker personal training: jp@cafitness.co.uk
Production: Bridget Fish, Vincent Smith

The publishers would like to thank Adrian George.
Every effort has been made to trace the copyright holders at the time of
going to press. We apologise for any unintentional omission and would be
pleased to insert the appropriate acknowledgement in all subsequent editions.

Text © Janet Street-Porter 2008
Design & layout © Quadrille Publishing Ltd 2008

Cataloguing in Publication Data: a catalogue record for this book is
available from the British Library

ISBN 978 184400 5864

Printed and bound in Germany

LIFE'S TOO F***ING SHORT

A guide to getting what you want out of life without wasting time, effort or money

JANET STREET-PORTER

QUADRILLE